# THE HEART WANTS WHAT IT WANTS:

*A Destined Twin Flame Journey*

An Autobiography by:

D.M. Batten

DIVINE WORKS PUBLISHING, LLC.
ROYAL PALM BEACH, FLORIDA

**ISBN:** 978-1-949105-59-9 (hardback)
**ISBN:** 978-1-949105-52-0 (paperback)
**ISBN:** 978-1-949105-53-7 (eBook)

First Edition Published: 03/06/2024
Printed in the United States

### Published by:

Divine Works Publishing
Royal Palm Beach, Florida USA
561-990-BOOK (2665)

*www.DivineWorksPublishing.com*

# Dedication

*To God,*

*Through you, all things are possible.*

*Love and Light.*

# Endorsements

*The Heart Wants What it Wants: A Destined Twin Flame Journey* is a big-hearted, heartbreaking and brave tale of one woman's quest for belonging and love. Floating multiple relationships, states and enough pop culture references to signify a life fully lived, Dolores Batten—a Sylvia Plath scholar—speaks to us in plainspoken, clever prose. She leaves, it seems, no memories unturned. Forget the author's orientation—her story, in the Borgesian sense, appeals to all humans in its search for the thing itself. *"If I could hug this voice, I would, many pages over."*

—Alex Z. Salinas,
Author of *Hispanic Sonnets* and *City Lights From the Upside Down*

With tenderness and sharp wit, *The Heart Wants What it Wants: A Destined Twin Flame Journey,* takes readers on a wild and winding journey as she lives and loves in the 1990's south. Amongst a chorus of sex, drugs, and rock-n-roll, Batten recounts her passions, addictions, lovers, and brushes with death in raw and vulnerable prose. She reminisces on the delights and discoveries that make her who she is today, reminding us that *"all we have is our moments."* This book will make you want to take a midnight swim with blue crabs, dance around the house to the Doors, and drink in the sticky-sweet Florida air. The adventures and misadventures of an endearing misfit, Batten's story is one of longing, and above all else, love.

—Sarah Alcaide-Escue
*Bruised Gospel*

When we come close to those things that break us down,

we touch those things that also break us open.

And in that breaking open,

we uncover our true nature.

-Wayne Muller

# Contents

# Acknowledgments

First off, I must thank Dr. Belinda John and the entire publishing team at Divine Works Publishing for seeing my vision for this book and bringing it to life. Our meeting was truly ordained by God.

To all of my friends, lovers, and soulmates, thank you for being a part of this journey, and for believing in me and supporting my mission here on earth. You have helped me become my best self in this life, and I am so blessed to know you.

To Jen, my twin flame, my eternal soul companion, my teacher, and my muse. I always promised that I would make us immortal. In spiritual truth, we always have been. Now we live on in the pages of this memoir. You are the best worst thing that ever happened to me and I love you endlessly with all of my heart. I, you, me, we—Love, D.

And to Jerri, my life partner, my soulmate, and my rock, you are the gift of God's love. You came to me when I needed a miracle, and you stood by me, unconditionally. Your love for me shines through our life together and your acceptance of my heart, and what it wants, is beyond human comprehension. Thank you, for helping to make my dreams come true, and for loving me so fearlessly—Your sweet pea.

Finally, to my dear grandmother Mildred. You truly are *Unforgettable*. It has been an honor living my life to make you proud, and in God's image, because they are truly one in the same. I was raised by an angel, and now I strive every day to live up to that legacy. I take with me the greatest lesson you taught me in this life: the most valuable riches in life are not made of money, they are made of love—Your little Dee Dee.

# Prologue

AUTOBIOGRAPHIES ARE ALL ABOUT CHOICE. You choose how much or how little to show of who you have been, and who you are. You wrap an experience beyond words (because it's *always* beyond words) into a neat little interwoven package with a pretty bow of your choice, spilling across the shiny edges—the shiny parts. You choose what goes in and what comes out; and you choose where the chapters of your life pause, change, and begin anew. You make the choice to break the binding of the book, and to set the words free—to be honest about what has happened in that space which you call life, and to marvel at its perceptions; its essence. But the choice to write an autobiography is not a choice at all. *It chooses you. It writes you.* Painting with colored words and bleeding hearts; raw emotions in the magic of its moonlight. I can take you on a voyage to my richest diamond-studded heavens or plunge you into the depths of my darkest hell. I can fly like a jet pilot, soaring above clouds, tumbling backwards, spiraling through language laden canyons, and end up on the right side of all of my wrongs. Or I can expose the fuselage altogether and let the fuel burn bright in its embers; burn... until nothing is left but the remnants of a charred black box.

# Chapter 1

## In the Beginning...

### Condensing My Past into a Small Snapshot

People often begin their autobiographies with long, drawn-out recounts of their early childhood years. I, personally, find this to be a sheer waste of paper. In an attempt to simplify the convoluted, I'll sum up the pertinent things you should know of my early years. I wound up in a body cast at the tender age of six months with no clue as of how I ended up in one, other than my aunt went to change my diaper one day, and I screamed bloody murder. Infuriated, she threatened to call my dad's mom, my grandmother Millie whom you will endearingly read more about within these pages. My aunt demanded I be taken to a hospital immediately. Then, amazingly enough, at midnight, my grandmother received a so-called "anonymous" call which relayed the truth of my abused condition. My grandmother's response? To promptly send a round trip ticket up to my hometown in New Jersey, and to have me brought to her immediately. I arrived in Florida with my mom the next day. My ticket however, unlike that of my parents, would only be one-way.

I grew up in Florida. Avocados, the size of watermelons, adorned my backyard as I was afforded all the beautiful luxuries a house near the ocean provided. I attended a Christian preschool, lived a happy life, won numerous competitions and contracts in modeling, piano, and dance. By second grade, I was classified "Gifted" by the academic community of my elementary school. I was a happy child, with a middle-class lifestyle and made more friends outside of school than I could count. So why was it then, that by the time I was in the fourth grade, only two years later, that I would attempt to hang myself on the playground slide?

## Standing Up to (...and Falling Down From) a Bully

By the fourth grade, I realized what the word "bullying" meant, head-on. I was playing at a magical wonderland that had just been built across from my school called "The Creative Playground." It was an elaborately-designed outdoor play place with suspension bridges and wooden tunnels... and spiraling slides. I don't remember much about this day, other than climbing to the top of this slide, while one of my fellow "gifted" peers tied a noose in the jump rope that ended up around my head as the result of a dare. I remember the feel of the taut plastic around my neck, how it pressed indentations into my flesh, pulsating around my throat like a beating heart. And I remember falling to the sand-filled ground, after about two minutes, and by the grace of God, the rope broke and I landed on the earth's floor.

This was the beginning of several challenges I'd face at school. I often felt like an alien; an outcast, a misfit. My classmates had all witnessed my treetop-slide descent, but they were the same age as me—no one knew how to process it. Subsequently, and as a condition of treatment for my "suicidal tendencies," I was required to meet with a school counselor, three times a week. In a knotted twist of fate and by a not-so-wonderful coincidence, my *Gifted* teacher also worked as the school guidance counselor. Lovely.

Once the school year ended, my grandmother gave me a choice of three gifts: I could either have a brand-new puppy, take a trip to Walt Disney World in Orlando, or be enrolled in a private school. Dying to be away from the monsters who came up with such a fun and sadistic game as a hide-and-go-seek-suicide, I chose to enroll in the same Baptist-based private school which provided my previous preschool education. I became close friends with a few of my peers and found myself less ostracized. I was winning.

I should mention, at this point, that as an infant I was christened in a Presbyterian Church named Chapel by the Sea. I played piano for them on a regular basis and I attended Sunday school with the church religiously. This was my childhood religious denomination and the basis of my ever-lasting faith. However, the intensity of the school's religious conviction was new terrain. Baptists, it would turn out, are a much different type of Christian than Presbyterians. They live by a strict code which forbids any kind of music, film, or literature that references drugs, sex, and/or any other acclaimed taboo. But aside from weekly Wednesday church services at the school chapel and the pastor's strong penchant for corporal punishment, not too much happened there. What is important to note however, is the time that I spent on the basketball team at this extremely strict Christian school, and what it foreshadowed about my future—a life still unbeknownst to me.

## Court is Now in Session

By junior high, I joined the junior basketball team. Every day for two hours I ran suicides up and down the court under the direction of Angela, a beautiful woman with curly blond hair and devastatingly striking blue eyes. Like every young athlete, I dreamt of the day when I would be the star of my team. In all reality, most of my time was spent picking splinters out of my shorts, but on occasion, I scored a point or two and received a fanfare from the bleachers beyond.

I loved the feeling of being on a team. I relished the opportunity to become better at something. And I loved going on road trips, which were par for the course, because the only teams a private school can play are those from other private schools, and they would typically be located several hundred miles away. Climbing into the church van with my boombox and a cassette keyed up to the strictly forbidden tracks of 2 Live Crew's *"Me So Horny."* I would sing to the endless loop of moans and groans along with the rest of my team for hours on end, during the long ride to our next rival. Truth be told, I didn't even truly know what I was listening to, only that the group had been banned in Florida for their excessively explicit lyrics about women and sex, and at that age, anything that you aren't supposed to listen to is the proverbial basis of what you *want* to listen to. These tapes, along with a multitude of religiously-banned media that I once owned, would later end up melting in the blaze of a burning inferno that I would set afire in my backyard, during the self-initiated purging of my own media in the name of God.

During the regular playing season one of my teammates, Sylvie, was kicked off the team and booted out of the school for reasons that no one would explain. It was an unspoken understanding. That is why, when we hopped in the van for an away game a week later, I couldn't figure out why Angela had stopped at Sylvie's house during the middle of a school day and picked her up to join us.

Throughout the ride to and from the game, Angela and Sylvie seemed to be very friendly. Sylvie was sitting shotgun to Angela and holding her hand during the entire drive. They would laugh at quiet jokes and wink at whispers that they shared, leaning their heads on each other while the rest of the team, tucked away safely in the back of the van, was doing their own thing. I should explain that Angela graduated the previous year and Sylvie was a senior. The math in this may seem confusing, as I was only in junior high, but it is explainable; in a rural town, the primary and secondary schools are blended into one. One school, one team. Go Eagles!

A few weeks later, I was in my mandatory chorale class, and got stuck at a long table, sitting next to Ricky, the resident school delinquent. While singing our arpeggios for the day, the teacher walked by and saw a carving on the wooden desk in front of the space between Ricky and myself. It simply read *"Angela is a Dyke."* She quickly sent both Ricky and I to the front office, and that is when the fun really began.

*While we wait for Ricky to finish up in the principal's office, I should tell you that Angela, the basketball coach, was also the pastor/headmaster's daughter. I didn't even put the two facts together until I was being paddled with a wooden plank which had been accented with decorative quarter-size holes which were there to make the whole process even more enjoyable and helped to leave a lasting impression—the one on my heart and my skin.*

Fast forward to fifteen minutes later and Ricky has been kicked out of the school. My turn. As I sat in the office, I cried out my innocence, coming within a razor's edge from getting kicked out of school myself. I was suspended for the rest of the week and given a strong warning that I must never say anything like that again. As I was waiting outside the office for my grandmother to come pick me up, who else but Angela came walking down the hall. I ran up to her and pleaded.

"Angela, I had nothing to do with that. I would never say that about you." She wiped my eyes with the bottom of her shirt and pulled me into a warm embrace. "It's ok, Dolores. I know *you*, of all people, would never say that."

I was ecstatic that she believed me. What I wasn't so sure about, however, was why she emphasized that *"I, of all people, wouldn't say that."*

I looked Angela straight in the eyes, and softly spoke. "I, I don't understand..." Her answer to me was quite simple: "Don't worry baby, some day you will."

## The Importance of Junior High School

When the year was over, I decided to change schools again, and attend a regular junior high school. I thought, after being a student with friends at Brevard Christian, the entire world of teenagers would change with me. This, sadly, could not have been further from the truth. The only four things I can remember of the entire three years are as follows:

**First**: I got kicked out of my History class one day and sent to sit in the hallway. A boy I knew, Jacob, told me he wanted me to give him head. I ran to the girl's bathroom and locked the door, but he slipped over the other toilet stall, climbed over the partition, and whipped it out. Wow, my first penis. I ran down the hallway again, this time screaming, and he slipped away like the flaccid snake that he had and that he *was*.

**Second**: I remember getting drunk in my chorale class. I was the lead pianist and had recently been made aware by the director that I possessed perfect pitch. This, of course, made the class warm-ups insulting. I did not need them. Instead, what I really needed was a juice box, filled up with Vodka, taped at the bottom and left over from the other day when I went to the neighboring church with the "cool kids" and smoked cigarettes without inhaling before sneaking back onto the cement track during my physical education class, just seconds before roll call.

**Third**: I enjoyed freestyle rapping in the courtyard with African American children and got used to being told that I was a "wigger." Trying to figure that word out gave me a headache. 'I am a person with rhythm and who holds a passion for the English language and the way words rhyme...' I thought to myself. I was colorblind. That is the nature of children, before they are tainted by the racial and gender biases of both the media and society at large. They do not see color and barely see gender, aside from that which is demarcated by body parts. They are born neutral into a prejudiced and hostile world.

**Fourth**: I also remember attending my Junior High prom and dancing with all the boys. Although they acted as if they did not like me during the school year, when it came to this dance, I was bumping and grinding with every last one of them. And I was idolizing the girls. One girl. An Italian goddess named Gina Tallerigo.

## The Innocence of Childhood

I didn't understand it then, as I may only partially understand it now, but I can tell you about Gina from the eyes of what a twelve-year-old sees. 'She's beautiful. She has a boyfriend who is a jerk, and she is very sweet to me during class. I want to spend more time with her. I want to be her friend. I think she should lose her boyfriend. I think she is amazing. I love the way she smells...and her eyes...and her lips. She has perfect lips...' I was infatuated, so much so, that when she casually invited me to her birthday party, I rode my bike a distance over forty miles to the all-ages 69 Boyz show at Club Marz where she would be that very night. I didn't know what to call it yet, but this was not like any friendship I had been longing for before.

In a time without cell phones and about an hour after I was expected home, I was pulling my bike up to a payphone down the street from where she lived. She gave me the physical address but I couldn't find my way there. After riding around for a few more hours, I tried to call again, but her phone line was busy. This is when I decided to just keep going, hoping to make it to the club by the time she got there.

I ended up running out of steam about another hour later, just in time to run into another kid I hung out with in school named Chris. He was at a local grocery store with his dad, and I convinced him to go to the club with me. His dad loaded my bike into the back of their pickup, and I was finally on my way.

I spent a few hours at Chris's house, letting him in on my plans, just how much I wanted to see Gina, and having him help me get my outfit just right, considering I had been riding with it underneath my play clothes for several hours. We went to a baseball card shop and I attempted to sell the cards that I had in my back pocket so I could buy a gift for the girl who made me feel so special.

Although I never made a pass at Gina, I felt differently about her. She was this girl who I wanted to be close to, and I despised her boyfriend Dominick. When Chris and I arrived at the club, Gina and I's heartfelt hug was abruptly interrupted with my arm being grabbed by my grandma's friend Misty and her son Derrick, as they drug me out of the room and drove me back home to my grandmother, all the while lecturing me for running away. Little did they know that I really wasn't running away from, but rather running towards something—a feeling I had yet been unable to internalize. The beating of my own heart.

# Sleeping with the Same Team

I spent the early years of my elementary and junior high life engaged in slumber parties; cuddling up with ten of my nearest and dearest 'girl' friends. Of course, there were "no boys allowed" at our weekly soirees. What on earth could a group of young girls do without boys? Especially, when these young girls had no interest in makeup like their older sisters, or any real desire to hang out with the boys at all? They could play doctor, just the same, and if years later someone called them out on it, they could easily shrug it off as an innocent childhood game. It is for this very reason that I found myself hiding in closets, huddled under blankets, and rolling on the floor naked with all of my female friends—all in the name of "kids will be kids."

Like the day when I was about nine. I was hanging out with my friend Heidi, whom my grandmother would later find laying on top of me in a closet. Both of us sky clad, kissing, and each of us with a fever that surpassed experimentation. But as my grandmother threw a pair of shorts at me and ran out the door, I could hear her mumbling in an exasperated tone "kids will be kids."

Or the time when I was close with a friend who my piano teacher introduced me to, Jillian, who I barely messed around with, as she was not into that. One evening, a few years later, when I was about eleven, her sister called me out of the blue and invited me over. That night we took things to the extreme; intense moaning with a pillow over my head. All I really remember is waking up naked next to her the next morning, bright and early, when her mom stood calling at the door, "Breakfast is ready! I made pancakes." And Fiona and I, scrambling to put our clothes back on, sitting at the table with her two brothers in a shared silence and with smirks on our faces. We knew. But hey, "kids will be kids."

Or even the pseudo love affair that I carried out with my best friend Chennelle, a gorgeous French girl who was my next-door neighbor for almost a decade. It wasn't until my teens that we realized all of the fooling around and experimenting we did with each other on endless sleepover weekends was a part of a bigger need: my lesbianism and her bisexuality.

But nothing can top the time when I had a birthday slumber party at my house and ALL the girls came over. As we spent the evening experimenting with one another, one girl—my next-door neighbor Holly—decided she did not want to be a part of our escapades and promptly ran home to inform her mother of our activities, referring to them as "lesbian orgies." Her mother came storming over moments later, claiming we were trying to give her daughter AIDS, an allegation we all vehemently denied. "How would that even be possible? What is wrong with that girl?" My grandmother's reply? You guessed it. "Kids will be kids."

# Chapter 2

# Coming Into the World

## Caught in the Middle

When I started high school, my sexual identity was still unknown to me. All I was certain of was that I had a new boyfriend named Kenneth, whom I met on the steps of the high school while I skipped my after-school rehearsal for the High School Chorale. He would be the one to take my flowering heterosexually-defined virginity. We carefully found opportunities to be together, and snuck away for our first sexual experience during the full moon of a Halloween night.

It was about six o'clock in the evening. I was dropped off at a Halloween party being hosted at the house of my Chorale director. Kenneth's mom, being an unknowing accomplice to our sexual awakenings, picked me up from the party and dropped us off at Wendy's to have a quick dinner date together. Little did she know, we had no intention of eating food, only each other. We wanted to be alone, so we walked across the street to the high school and sat on the football bleachers. I was dressed provocatively in a costume I cannot remember, only that it required pantyhose. I remember him slipping them off my feet, moments before I grabbed onto the hard metal bench while he and I slowly delved into the blossoming expressions of teen-age lust.

Even though I didn't love him, I was willing to try. Later in the week, however, I would instead run off with Jeff, a beautiful twenty-four year old who I was enamored with. Even though Kenneth and I had recently perused engagement rings at the local Sears, Jeff trumped Kenneth when he handed me an envelope one night with a small uncut diamond inside. I was falling for this man and decided to see where it would go.

We started out as an innocent couple, just killing time together. He was hot, I was hot... it was hot! I felt attracted to him and all the freedom he enjoyed that I as a high school freshman, could not. I would spend many days at his house, skipping school over the train tracks, making out with him; touching, feeling, tasting, exploring. We would always stop right before, usually ending with him pleasing me orally, engaging ourselves in virtually every sexual situation possible except actual sex.

One morning, instead of skipping school to see him like I usually did, I decided that I wanted to be with him once and for all. I was going to run away. Jeff and I met up early in the morning, and walked off the school grounds, intent on starting a new life together. We ran through two differ-ent counties, during a day of endless walking and occasional hitchhiking, in which I shed several pounds, along with my clothes on several occasions. Our actual first time happened in the woods, during a simple rest from our long walk. Jeff laid me down on a bed of leaves, his body hovering over me. As I tugged at his belt, he asked me, like a true gentleman, "Are you sure you wanna do this?" The reaching around of both my hands and legs gave him his answer. "Yes."

Jeff was a demigod of beauty. Handsome rugged features with dirty blond hair and sparkling blue eyes. (To this day, he is the most attractive man that I have ever been with). However, this journey was not without concern. One day, while Jeff was out getting groceries for the house we were crashing at, I found myself curious. Looking through his suitcase, I found discharge papers from the hospital. He had been having some type of kidney problems and what looked like blood tests that hadn't come back yet. My mind railed against the possibility that he could have AIDS. But, in the heat of the moment, I couldn't let that concern me. What was done was already done. I neatly tucked the paperwork back inside his suitcase, and that was the last I thought about it. At least for now. Jeff and I spent a few nights at his friend's house in Vero before ending up at a house party in which we couch surfed the remaining two nights away. However, after spending a grand total of five days of making love to and harboring a minor, Jeff was unable to keep us together. His friends told him that they were going to call the cops, as they had seen my picture on a missing person's ad on TV—the equivalent of the proverbial missing child on the milk carton. After begging him from a bathtub bubble bath and pleading with him through the lyrics of Boyz II Men's "Down on Bended Knee," we left the party house and walked to a payphone. Jeff kissed me goodbye as he dialed the number to the local police department. I was still high on the adrenaline of the night, when my grandmother walked into the police station and dragged me out to the car—this is where my carriage would become a pumpkin once again. I spoke to Jeff one last time that night, when he called the house to make sure I got home okay. And that was the last time I heard from my Eros.

## Trying to Straighten Out the Not

Broken-hearted and empty-handed, a few months later, I also slept with my friend, James—on pure impulse. One day before school, as we were smoking a cigarette in the back of the Walgreens store, the vice principal came barreling through the parking lot in a truck with a handheld loud-speaker and announced that he would be suspending anyone not on school grounds. James and I ran like our lives depended on it, finally finding ourselves in a small barricade of boxes that had been set out behind the store. We ducked into this sanctuary just moments before the truck came speeding by. To stay hidden, we had to lie on top of each other, pressed against one another like hot metal, soldered together by the morning sun. As we lay there, trying to take our mind off the imminent danger of being caught, we began to kiss. Passionately. We found out that morning what a challenge it is to remove your clothes without being able to move positions under a cascade of boxes.

James was sweet and being with him was comforting. A few years later, I would even date him for a while. Only, I wasn't there for the relationship thing, I liked the way he felt holding me, and he knew how to touch me and make me respond. We were there for each other as a means of sexual convenience. He and I were both getting good at what we were doing, even though, truth be told, we didn't have any business doing *what we were getting good at* with each other in the first place.

# Chapter 3

# The End of the Beginning

## Take Me Out to the Ballgame Built for Two

Later that year, my grandma received a letter from my dad. Turns out he was painting a white porcelain toilet red with the blood that was now trickling from the sides of his mouth. His diagnosis of lung cancer came after a prolonged lapse in judgment in which he refused to follow-up on his less-menacing skin cancer. Now, during the most formative years of my life, it was time to sell the house, surrender my puppy Ginger Marie to the Humane Society, and move back to New Jersey. The man whom I never had known as my father beyond his three small childhood visits, was dying.

On the plus side, at least my dad and I could finally spend some quality time together. Three more times, to be exact. A crack of a baseball bat, the thunderous boom of rubber hitting the three-point line, the whip of a football, and he was gone. Less than six months stood between me finally being a part of my dad's life, and then being a part of his twenty-one-gun salute. Final. The end. Fin.

I had experienced death before. My aunts had passed away, and I had already been to a few funerals. Back then, all I had were questions. I didn't have any of those now. All I had was a hole in my life that had just been filled, only to be dug up again. This time, flowers grew on that covered hole and my dad's lifeless body lay beneath it.

Meanwhile, back at the school front, I had been trying to make a few friends, using my usual methods of drinking, smoking, and basically acting a fool. I found one friend who seemed to be worth having; her name was Diana. The trouble was, I just wanted a friend. Meanwhile, she and her boyfriend fancied a threesome. With my dad's death still fresh on my mind, the last thing I wanted was to feel like a piece of meat. I told my grandmother about their indecent proposal and she whisked us away to the other end of the country; Georgia. Home of the Sweet Peach. I would soon find out that for me, the state's nickname would be an exercise in double entendre.

## The Trouble with Georgia Peaches

This is where my life truly began. I hung out with a group of friends who were absolute misfits. Techno grunge industrial goths with a passion for music and a love of being different. I met my best friend, Shawn, through Mara, a girl in one of my classes. While enjoying our regular outings of misadventures, I found music. Or rather, it found me. I fell in love with a little Swiss Alpine Village CD shop in the downtown area of the small Georgian town which specialized in techno and industrial music. I also found a wonderful little coffee shop, in which I met many mystics who gave me a deep appreciation for the world and the writings of Buckland, Cunningham, Bruce, and Cage.

One of the best moments of my teenage Georgia experience was my first local band concert, Phantasmagoria. I went with my group of misfits and my boyfriend at the time, Adam. This is where I first met Bree, a gorgeous black-haired, blue-eyed girl, who flashed her tits for a random camera while she stared at me and laughed, holding her shirt just a little longer than necessary, many seconds past the glimmer of a flashing light.

A few weeks later, I attended a birthday party for Mara, and both Bree and Adam were there. As soon as we got there, Adam and I went upstairs and made out in Mara's bed. I can still remember the feeling of kissing this boy; a real kiss, unlike my first kiss in junior high, in which a boy with gum in his mouth unleashed a sword fight on my tonsils. With Adam, who was a total hottie, it was fun, but awkward. Nothing clicked. No magic. Why was there never any magic? Even with Jeff, I was more into the sensation than the man. Although he was hot, I never felt true love for him. I would soon find out why.

When it was time to leave the party, Shawn offered to drop me off at home. Bree came out and told Shawn that she had to run a quick errand, so we waited for her, bundled up in twenty-degree weather, smoking cigarettes in his blue Ford Escort sedan. As I stared at the snow-covered mountains that stretched out in front of us, he leaned over to me and whispered "She likes you. She wants you to spend the night at her house."

I smiled. "That's great," I said. "I like her too. She seems like an awesome person!"

"No, I don't think you get it. She *LIKES* you," he repeated. I thought over this statement for a second, and all I could come up with was "*I LIKE* her too, Shawn. I'd love to hang out at her house."

Shawn shook his head and responded, "You don't understand what I'm trying to tell you, but you will..."

#TheHeartWantsWhatItWants

# Chapter 4

# It's All About the Journey

## The Road to Becoming Me

When Bree hopped back into the car, I was all about it. I told her I would love to have a slumber party, and so Shawn dropped me off at Bree's house. The night went on forever, as we sat and listened to music and got to know each other. As the moon crept high into the sky, Bree asked me to play a game. An adaptation of "Truth or Dare" which she affectionately named "Truth or Truth." The idea was that, with her parents right upstairs, it would be next to impossible to take any dare worth doing. I agreed. Hours passed finding out tidbits about our lives under the true sentiment that honesty was the sacrament that held the game together and kept it from becoming boring.

It was about three in the morning, and Bree was up to bat with her question. I remember sitting up on the bed, with Bree right beside me. She slides over to me a little, puts a hand against my leg, and asks "Have you ever kissed a woman?" I pause for a moment, not sure how to answer this or even why I was being asked. "No." I responded. The truth is I hadn't. All those years of playing doctor didn't count, because we never acknowledged that it meant anything. Remember, "kids will be kids..."

She waited a few moments to glide herself into a repeat of the question.

"So, would you ever want to?"

I felt flushed—my hands sweaty, my throat dry; my body burning like a flame had been placed inside of it. Amidst the closed doors, the fire had nowhere to go. I think quickly.

"I would, but my throat and my lips are dry." 'Good save,' I thought to myself.

But Bree calls my bluff. She jumps up like a jackrabbit and runs into the bathroom. Moments later, she comes back with a glass of water. Walking over to the stereo, she turns on the first track of a techno CD by Lords of Acid: "VooDoo-U": an electronica masterpiece with hypnotizing vocals and penetrating bass. As the lead singer croons: *"The magic is in the feeling, I can make you do what I want you to,"* I find myself enraptured. That's when Bree weaves her way up to me, straddles me, and binds both of my hands with one of hers. Pushing me onto the bed and pouring the water down my throat, I feel as if I am about to drown, until she dabs her fingers into the glass, rubbing them gently against my lips. Minutes pass by like years, until she breaks the silence once more.

"So, do you want to...?"

I have no outs at this point, my excuse having failed me. I resign to her will.

"Sure."

Have you ever felt the sensation of free falling? Of time standing still and the world feeling perfect and immense and infinite? This is what it felt like. From the first moment that her lips pressed against mine, I finally felt that thing I was searching for. I felt free. As I continued to run my tongue against her lips and to slide the shirt over her head, I slowly came to the realization that I was feeling it, but it wasn't because *she* liked girls... it was because *I* did.

She slowly, slow-ly... ever... so... slow...ly..., ran her finger-tipped magic down every inch and curve of me. She kissed every facet of my face, my neck, my breasts; all the way down to my stomach. Pause. I looked up at her, my mouth watering, my lips parted and sighed softly, letting out a gentle moan, all the while just trying to breathe but forgetting how.

All I could see now was the polished silver chrome of her belt buckle, as my body lay beneath it. Panic washed over me like endless waves brushing upon the shore, as I became shrouded in the dueling fear and the exhilaration of the unknown. 'What in the world was I doing? Why did I have to start thinking about it? Could it be that I *want* to think about it?' Bravely, I ran my hands along her belt, slipping my fingers into the loops. Feeling the cold metal of the buckle beneath my fingertips. Fumbling with the prong. Lightly tugging at the strap.

Suddenly, her body collided with mine, moving rhythmically, drawing me further into the moment. And as we moved together, I could feel myself becoming one with her. But then, abruptly, it came to an end. Just as quickly as it had begun, it was over. At that moment, I looked into her eyes with a gentle and vulnerable gaze. I traced my hand slowly up the side of her breast, to her face, and tenderly kissed her before rolling away from her. As I lay there beside her, breathing heavily, my mind filled with awe as I contemplated the significance of what had just transpired. We lay there for a while, my hand gently grazing hers. I couldn't speak or think. All I could do was feel.

I spent moments suspended in a wondrous daze, until I worked up my nerve, slowly, to return to her. On my own. I took charge of these feelings that I was trying so desperately to suppress, and I leaned in and kissed her again. I slid my body on top of hers this time, fully conscious that this was NOT playing doctor; that I could not rationalize my way out of this. I kissed her deeply, sliding my tongue into her mouth, running my fingers over every inch of her. I devoured her body, caressing her breasts with the eagerness of Christmas. Her body was mine for the taking. Her devious smile revealed that she had awakened something inside of me that could no longer be contained. She had awakened me.

As we got back into that groove and I felt my hand slide under the metal sliver that held the belt together in its notch, I paused again. Even though

I was dying to feel her, my brain kept screaming "Damnet! I can't...", and I moved my hand back, and this time, she smiled and sat up. Her next words cut like daggers through my newly exposed heart.

"This can never happen again. I am not into girls, but I knew you were and wanted to help bring you out of the closet. *Everybody knows.*"

How in the world could *everybody* know something that I am not even aware of? What about me is so revealing to others, yet continues leaving me in the dark?

"I just wanted to make you see it for yourself." she continued.

What?! What on earth has this woman done to me? Mind fucked and alone, although I am only inches from her. I curl into a ball and try to sleep but I can't. All I want now is to be close to her, inside of her, to rip her belt off with my teeth. Something must be wrong with me! I mentally run through a grocery list of sexual denials: 'I have a boyfriend.' 'I'm not a virgin.' 'I want to get married someday.' 'I'm a Christian, for God's sake... For His sake, literally!'

What is happening to me?

## Love (or Something Like It)

I feel like I'm falling in love. That must be what I feel. Wanting something that I never wanted before, knowing that I was doing the same thing with past boyfriends that I had just done with her, and the only difference is that I was emotionally numb when I was in a boy's arms. With her, I had been awakened. I was renewed. I felt *alive*.

I entered the school lunchroom the next day with anticipation, eager to join my friends as usual. You see, our group of outcasts, of which I was fortunate to belong, gathered every morning before class to chat, enjoy our meals, and tell jokes. As I took a seat beside Shawn, Bree decided to move from her usual spot beside us and instead opted for a chair at the table's end. I looked over at her and realized that she was ignoring me. It took everything inside of me to not blurt something stupid out like "I think I love you." Too bad that everything inside me was *still* not enough to keep me from saying it. As

I boldly made my love declaration in front of the entire table, Bree simply looked at me with scornful eyes and uttered, "Get over it."

Over the next few months, as I stood by the bus stop or sneaked out for cigarettes, day after day, I would bring along my Walkman CD Player and wear my headphones. I found solace in listening to Jars of Clay's "Sinking" on repeat. Despite the fact that this song falls under the genre of Christian Rock, I firmly believed that it was my prerogative to enjoy it, as my love for God remained unwavering. I felt the song had a double meaning. My attempt to avoid loving Bree because she was a woman, and my attempt to continue to be a child of God, although I felt that if I *was* a lesbian He would turn His back on me forever and I would be damned. Wait a minute. Did I just say that? Am I a lesbian?

#TheHeartWantsWhatItWants

# Chapter 5

# Crash and Burn

## What Goes Up, Must Come Down

Since my dreams of being with Bree were crushed, I trudged along, class after class; running into Mara in English, breaking up with Adam in History, and having Bree avoid eye contact with me in the busy hallways between classes. I was out in the deep. How on earth could the same woman who shared such an intimate moment in time with me now act as if I didn't exist? I didn't know what to do, so I did the only thing I could do: I wrote. I wrote love letters, every day; sometimes sliding them into her locker, other times handing them to Shawn to give to her. Deep poems of love unrequited. This newfound passion surging through me turned me into a poetry beast. I would write constantly, from sun-up to sundown, finding creative ways to give her the letters. The letters that I still believed echoed deep down in her heart as she had echoed in mine.

Six months passed. Slowly, I stopped writing as many letters. However, I kept a small recipe box full of trinkets of the time we had shared together—a cigarette butt with her lipstick, a blossom of honeysuckle that she had picked and placed behind my ear when we were just innocent friends, before the infamous moment that changed my life forever.

Meanwhile, Shawn remained close friends with Bree. They were best friends before I moved to Georgia; Shawn was now my best friend, too. After endless months of Bree's rejection, I had just about given up when, out of the blue, I received a call from Shawn inviting me to come swimming with him, Bree, and her friend. My heart pinged, just a little, as I reservedly asked, "Will she mind?" Shawn replied "No, but you have to be cool. Give her space. Just be cool."

"Okay," I gushed. 'I can do that,' I thought to myself. Shawn picked me up and we drove to a pool where Bree and Shawn's male friend Mike were already swimming. I jumped out of the car, bathing suit clad, and cannonballed into the water. I swam by myself for a while, sneaking glances at Bree, and even though she remained cold towards me, something in her eyes gave the slightest hint of forgiveness. I was forgiven for falling in puppy love with her.

# Bree Revisited 2.0

We spent the rest of the afternoon hanging out like nothing ever happened. I was careful not to bring anything up, not to come too close. After we dropped Shawn's friend off, Bree made plans to hang out with Shawn for the rest of the evening. I wanted so desperately to invite myself, but fearing another rejection, I stepped outside of the car, waved goodbye, and walked towards my front door. Suddenly, as if in slow motion, Bree called out to me, saying she had a present for me. I smiled. A gift, from her: maybe a letter, explaining what she was truly feeling, or a trinket of some sort, just something showing she hadn't forgotten about me. That she still cared.

I turned to receive the "gift" and found myself in a warm embrace. Bree bent me completely backwards and began to make out with me voraciously; passionately. While I was in the moment, my grandmother opened the front door and found me standing there, my tongue buried in Bree's mouth, my arms wrapped around her so tightly that I truly thought the jaws of life could not wrench us apart. Unfortunately for me, my grandmother could. She pulled us apart, using flattened boxes from our move as a barrier against the door, and as she slammed it shut with me inside, Bree began to scream through my window. "I am so sorry for what I put you through. I love you and I want to be with you. I want to take you home and eat you for dinner." Done. I jumped to the window, trying to pry it open, as my grandmother came barreling through the room and blocked my window first with flattened boxes; I fumbled with the lock which was stuck, and she returned with a nail and hammer, foiling my escape plan. She screamed at Bree to leave and then proceeded to call her parents and advise them that their daughter had just kissed me on the front porch of our home.

Oh my God. I finally get this opportunity to finish what we had started months ago, and here my grandmother is crushing OUR love and MY chances. "Dear God, why is this happening to me?" I pleaded to myself, as I walked from my room to the living room; the space where Bree's mother would soon stand, frantically irate.

## Dolores, You Got Some 'Splaining to Do

My grandmother asked everyone to take a seat. Bree joined her mom on the couch, while grandmother and I picked separate chairs. As she recounted what she witnessed to Bree's mom, Bree's eyes meet mine. She slowly moves her legs, revealing that she was not wearing any panties under her skirt. 'Lord help me... seriously' I think to myself. My first view of her soft rose petals, vapors clouding my mind; I hear nothing. I know they are talking about us, but all I can think about is what would have happened if my grandma simply hadn't come to the door. I would have jumped back into the car, driven far away with Shawn, and made love to Bree, a woman, somewhere, anywhere, my thirst finally quenched for the first time.

At this point, Bree's mother looks at her and says "Bree, give me your purse." Bree looks up, and small tears fill her eyes as she reluctantly hands the bag over. Soon I would know why. Her mother then proceeds to dump the purse onto our coffee table, and every letter, every flower, everything I had ever given her, came crashing down, along with my dreams. Her mother then continued "your granddaughter is sixteen and Bree is only fourteen. If Dolores ever comes near my daughter again, I am going to press charges for statutory rape."

*"What? I didn't rape anyone. I didn't do anything wrong. I didn't even have sex with her. I just love her,"* I thought to myself as her mom stormed out. Bree turned her head one last time and mouthed "I'm sorry," before being dragged by her arm out the front door and out of my life forever.

# Chapter 6

# Pain Personified

## The Stuff I Don't Like to Talk About

There was yet another man in my life during this time too. Jonathan. After being in so much pain over Bree and trying to regain some semblance of a normal straight life during my pining, I found myself in the arms of another man. Remembering how we met or how long we stayed together is an unimportant blur. What I do remember is how I turned from saint to sinner, and how I paid dearly for it.

Jonathan's mom had a special room that we were never allowed to enter. One night, after Jonathan fell peacefully into slumber with me wrapped up at his side after a session of meaningless and unfulfilling sex, I wandered my way into this room with his best friend Derrick. The room was laid out like the old jungle gyms on the playground, and in the middle, a bed, suspended by chains. A large stereo system was stationed in the corner of the room. Its speakers were attached to parts of the bed, and the whole thing moved. Amazing! Jonathan had never shown me the power of this room, so, while he lay sleeping, his friend Derrick was all too willing to give me the grand tour.

Sex with him felt incredible. Not because I was finally enjoying being with a boy, but because the room was dancing, and I was riding the waves of this musically throbbing pleasure running through the chains while riding him. Bass thudded into my spine, creating large waves of enjoyment, as I became one with the music and forgot all about who I was sharing it with. All I knew was that it felt good, being contained, held tightly by a suspended cage, my hands wrapped around the bars, my wrists tied in chains, while Derrick plotted his own course to ecstasy through a bass-filled orgasm.

When I awoke from my post-orgasmic daze, I wandered into the living room, buttoning my fly, and Derrick grabbed a beer before retreating outside. I felt good. I enjoyed a moment few would ever experience. I felt as if I had unlocked some huge secret, and even though I felt nothing for this lover, I felt fulfilled by the rush of music that enraptured my soul.

As I sat on the couch to write Bree a love-note, holding onto the orgasm I had just experienced as a catalyst of a sexual fantasy involving her that I had yet to embark on, Jonathan's other friend Squirrel pulled up a seat next to me. He began brushing the hair out of my eyes and went in to kiss me. 'I don't need this...' I thought to myself. I already felt guilty for sleeping with one of Jonathan's friends and for breaking into his mom's secret room. Little did I know that I would feel this guilt for the next decade of my life, but not for the reasons that you might suspect.

I gently pushed Squirrel's hand away, expecting him to get up and leave. He didn't. He grabbed my face forcefully and started kissing me. I pulled hard to get away and he threw me down to the floor. His eyes were razor sharp, like that of a wolf. I went to move from him but he pinned me underneath him. Then he pulled out a knife. Pressing the knife to my throat, he began to undress me, against my will. I softly pleaded "No," but he wouldn't listen. He knew exactly what he wanted and he was willing to take it by force. To take me by force. He ripped my jeans down and slid inside me violently. Even though I had just finished having sex with Derrick, it hurt worse than anything I had ever experienced. His hands were firm and gruff as he held me down and threw his full body weight into me. Over and over I told myself "I'm not here. This is a bad dream. Just a bad dream. I'm sound asleep with Jonathan, and everything is OK," but I couldn't make myself buy my own lies.

He finished with me and wiped himself before pushing my head into the carpet. "If you tell anyone about this, I will fucking kill you!" he growled, pulling his pants back up and walking to the fridge to grab a beer as if nothing had just happened. Tears formed in the ducts of my eyes, but I kept them at bay. '*I need to make it back downstairs and go to bed with Jonathan,*' I thought to myself. How I wished I had stayed there, safe in my boyfriend's arms, neither a cheater nor a rape victim. Just peaceful. I would not find that piece of me again anytime soon. I returned to bed with my boyfriend and lay awake with my eyes closed for hours, trying to wish away what had just happened.

## Dazed and Transgendered

I went about the next year confused and rather alone. Aside from Shawn, who seemed to have my back in everything except for coping with the rape that he did not know about, that I never spoke of. I was alone too much with my own thoughts. I spiraled into an all consuming depression. I became frigid to the idea of a relationship until Allison came around and changed my world perspective. She made me truly confront who I am, and the thought alone was exhilarating and terrifying, all at the same time.

I met Allison while she worked at Quiznos. She made the best sandwiches ever. She was cute and sweet, and Shawn knew how badly I had wanted a woman after Bree, so he proceeded to hook the two of us up. I should tell you, at this point, that Allison was transgendered. I had never met someone who had been a "he" who was working on becoming a "she" before. The idea intrigued me, but I never really saw Allison as anything other than a woman. She had adopted the name Allison in honor of Allison Rayne, a transgendered woman who had been tortured and killed for her sexuality.

That's a scary statement. Killed for being yourself. Murdered for not fitting into some stereotype of false gender, what Judith Butler deemed the "gender performance." I feared what that meant for me. I may be more accepted than her because two women together is a male fantasy, but there are still people in this world who hold so much hate for others that they would take a life simply because they did not agree with another person's free will. Is that what I had to look forward to for being a lesbian?

Regardless of my own insecurity, I went on a few dates with Allison. I remember eating ice cream cones together in the downtown shopping villa, where she would proceed to kiss me. Tenderly. I could feel her Adam's apple when I touched her neck. Her breasts were small as they pressed against my own chest. But none of this mattered. I liked her and that was that.

I learned a lot about transgender issues through this experience. She told me her story of transforming from Robert, as her driver's license still clearly stated, to Allison. She was on a regimen of hormone therapy treatments and was saving up for an operation that would allow her anatomy to match her heart and mind. The heart and mind of a woman.

One night, after one of our dates, I went back to her place. We started kissing on the couch, and it turned into more. We explored each other, softly, under the light glow of a television screen left on in a nearby room. I was doing fine, happy to be there with her, until I felt the throbbing hardness of her against my leg. She reached down to get undressed, and I freaked out. I jumped up from the couch and explained to her that I couldn't do this. I liked her and all, but this was too much. I'm sure the rape I never spoke of played a small part in the situation as well. I had not been with anyone since Squirrel... since that night, when I broke up with my boyfriend and ran far away from everyone and everything that I loved, even though I never left. Or shall I say the monsters never left me...

Allison walked me out to her car. When we arrived at my house, she said she wanted to talk to my grandmother and would not take no for an answer. *'Oh great! Just great'* I thought. *'Here we go again...'*

Up until this point, my grandmother had put all the responsibility of the kiss she witnessed between Bree and I on Bree. I was able to work around it by telling her I thought I might be bisexual, to which she responded, "Don't worry. It's just a phase."

*'Who's worried?'* I thought to myself. I knew what I wanted. I wanted to be with a woman. A full blown, fully sexually-equipped woman. Allison had been so close to what I was looking for that I was almost there again, in that moment that I needed, deep down in my soul, until her penis scared me away.

## When Things Go from Bad to Worse

Allison knocked on my grandmother's door, and as she answered, Allison walked in and headed straight for the coffee machine. *What the hell? She has never even been in my house before and now she is making herself coffee?'* I felt violated all over again.

"I need to tell you that your granddaughter is gay," she blurted out. All at once, the color rushed out of my face—it's presence replaced by a pale terror that Allison would expose everything I was in the process of still figuring out for myself. The last thing I wanted was to have this talk with my grandmother. I needed time to figure things out... To figure me out. I wanted to be sure and comfortable with who I am before telling the world—or the people that meant the world to me—my dark secret. Allison did not give me that opportunity.

Allison dedicated the next two hours to providing a comprehensive and excruciatingly detailed account. She covered everything, from my previous discussions about Bree to the intricacies of our own relationship. However, she conveniently omitted to mention that I refused engaging in sexual activities with her prior to her operation, despite her strong desire. This omission was, in fact, the root cause of her attempt to extort me as a form of revenge for rejecting her advances. Remarkably, this was the only aspect that this twenty-something-year-old woman neglected to mention in her relationship with a sixteen-year-old girl. Quite puzzling, one must admit!

As the night concluded, I felt totally exposed. Allison left my grandmother's house after the sun had just come up, and I sat on the couch, mortified of the imminent *"talk"* that I knew was coming. My grandmother looked hurt. She didn't say much, but that alone spoke volumes. I tried to distract myself with the television while the adults talked—until I felt that I had spent enough time under the microscope. "I'm tired," I said. Soon after, she left and I retreated off to bed. This was the last time I saw Allison and was the last time, for a while, that my grandmother and I had any conversation even *remotely* about my sexuality.

# Love's Interlude

I did get to see Bree one more time, the day before I left Georgia for good and traveled back to Florida, to our new home. I convinced my grandmother to drop me off at Shawn's to say a final goodbye, and then I proceeded to beg him to drive me over to Bree's. As I walked through her back-porch door and into the kitchen, Bree was standing by the refrigerator. She gave me a faint smile and told me to stay put. She came back moments later with a unicorn charm and placed it on the plain silver chain that I wore on my neck. She kissed me on the lips very briefly, very softly, and said "I'll never forget you. I love you. Goodbye." My heart shattered a second time, as I walked out that door—and Bree walked out of my life forever.

# Chapter 7

# Thinking with My Heart

## It's All About the Girl

Ileft for Florida shortly afterwards. I had not told anyone about the sexual assault. The rape of both my body and soul, which, even now, still haunts me. I held it in my heart like a bleeding cancer that slowly tore apart my happiness, forcing me into an uber-sexual state that positioned me to sleep with an excess of a hundred people over the next few years. But that comes later. First, I tackled the acceptance of my sexuality and coped with the aftermath of the assault on my own terms. Subsequently, numerous therapists would try to connect these two aspects, suggesting that a negative encounter with a man must have contributed to my attraction towards women. But truth be told, I wouldn't describe the consensual relations I had with men as bad, but rather lacking in emotional connection and not meeting my desired level of fulfillment. It is also worth noting that my relationship with Bree preceded the traumatic event, and my desires were already clear to me. I knew what I wanted. I wanted a woman. But you don't come out of the closet all at once, and you *definitely* do not claim yourself gay in the early nineties while living in the conservative mountain backwoods of Georgia.

Being back in Florida was like a time warp, only my grandma and I traded the luxury of the beach for the financial sensibility of the suburban landscape. The constant moving from Florida to New Jersey to Georgia and back drained whatever money was left in savings after the sale of our old house, and as such, grandma and I became first-time tenants of an apartment complex. One day, as a new resident, I went for a quick walk around my surroundings, and ran into a boy named Brian. He told me he lived on the third floor and to come visit him any time. I don't exactly remember how I said it, but I could tell that he was hitting on me, and with my newfound sexual identity, I wanted to be clear. "I'm bi" I told him. "Well shit, then you should definitely come over cuz' my friend is bi too and her and her girlfriend should be here any minute." I pondered the idea for a moment. *'Finally. I can meet someone who is actually into women and maybe feel some type of relief and support knowing that there are others like me.'*

I decided to take Brian up on his offer.

I waited upstairs, drinking a beer with Brian until there was a knock at the door. Two girls, about the age of eighteen, walked into the room; one who was not very responsive other than a nonchalant "hi" and the other... the other took my breath away. From the moment I met her, I knew that she was something special, someone that was meant to come into my life. Her name was Jen, and the girl with her was her girlfriend at the time, Michelle. I had never been in the presence of a bisexual couple, so I felt almost intimidated by them. Jen, however, must have seen through that nervousness, and made me feel at ease in her presence. I remember laying on the bed in Brian's room, this guy I had just met, while Jen and I chatted with each other, and then sitting on the edge of Brian's couch, exchanging witty comments and dangerously flirtatious glances with each other, while her girlfriend was in the other room, doing something that doesn't matter, because in that moment all that mattered was Jen; it was her presence in the first of many rooms that would fade into the background of what would become my life.

I felt her touch my hand and a spark arose between us; from the second we met, I was entranced. We were quite vocal in our mutual like of each other. I told her I thought she was hot. Her response, "You're not so bad yourself." The words she spoke flew off her lips like satin. This was accompanied by her beautiful long flowing black hair and piercing brown eyes that seemed to reach into my soul and extract every ounce of sensuality and sexuality that I possessed. I felt warm and light, floating on clouds, just to be around her. She was intoxicating.

We hit it off immediately, talking about who knows what as if we already knew each other. I could see the look of disdain in her girlfriend's eyes. She would pull Jen closer to her in some obviously intentional affection, meant to signal that I should back off. But how could I?

The next thing I remember was being in the car with Jen, Michelle, and Jen's friend Shane. As I glanced over, Jen's smile and demeanor said all the things I couldn't. I wanted so badly to kick the other girl out of the car, reach over, and kiss her. Hold her. Let myself be carried away by this wanton abandon and this incredible rush of pure feeling wrapped up in lust that enraptured my soul. I imagined spending the rest of the day with her during the car ride, wondering constantly if she was as taken by me as I was by her. But I said none of these things. Instead, I got out of the car at my apartment, and walked away.

I just walked away. I walked away. I walked-THE-FUUUCK-away. My heart racing, my hands clammy, and I went into my room where I would remain until later that evening, when I would return to Brian's apartment, secretly wishing that Jen had dropped off the girlfriend and came back over. No such luck. However, he told me she wanted me to have her phone number. That I should call her some time. I still remember the first time I did. She spent the next few days letting me in; opening up her world to me so that I could know everything about her. We talked for hours on end, from sun-up to sundown. Even though she constantly switched over to talk to Michelle, she would find any excuse to get off the phone with her and spend the rest of the night with me. She told me how she wanted out of the relationship she was in, and this just made me fall faster and deeper into the unknown.

As our friendship blossomed, she invited me over one night to watch a movie: "Sid and Nancy," a story all about the Sex Pistol's lead man, Sid

Vicious. At this point I should mention that Jen possessed this deeply dark side, attracted to 80's glam and heroin, and all the things that the rock stars of the mid-to-late-twentieth-century were all about. Just laying on her bed, next to her, was paradise. Although the details blur in my mind from years of life, and an endless supply of drugs taking their toll, I remember the way she looked in vivid detail; I remember the way that she felt pressed against me like it was yesterday; her sculpted body draped in a plain white cotton t-shirt that hugged her form, and light blue pajama bottoms clinging to her curves, and me, pressed against her body, leaning up from her stomach and kissing her for the first time. Several times. She, allowing me to be the aggressor, lying still beneath me. Ten minutes in, the movie was a far-off memory, even though it played on in the background. I remember running my hands along her body, her sides, and groping her breast, her nipple, while Nancy was yelling Sid's name. And then, just like it had begun... pause.

That's where it stopped.

*'Fuck fuck fuck fuck Fuck!'* I thought to myself. *'It's happening again.'* The last time I was here, in this type of moment with a woman who I was deeply attracted to, I choked. This time was different though; the timing felt off. I couldn't tell whether I was blowing it or if she just wasn't interested. We bonded so quickly, yet indefinitely, so penetratingly, but when it came to sealing the deal... crickets. The chemistry wasn't clicking. We didn't work. I was not ready to go there, and she was not making any moves in reciprocation. I frantically analyzed the situation in my head, dreading the thought that I may never get the opportunity again to be this close to her. We attempted to play it off, but in the back of my mind the gears were turning faster than I could keep up with. *'Why is it that, now, while I am with some beautiful woman that I just want to ravish, I pause, breakdown, and stop?'* I asked myself. I didn't like the answer that came to me, something so dark that I can only now bring it into the light.

After being raped in Georgia just six months prior, I began to have a huge Obsessive Compulsive Disorder. My torture scenario had to do with the recurring AIDS tests that I was taking at the time, as a result of both Jeff's illnesses and Squirrel's violation. I felt like my life might be doomed, a fact that was overly impressed upon me through the height of the AIDS epidemic during the 1990's, a time in which AIDS was a guaranteed death sentence. How in the world could I be with the first woman I was truly falling in love with, when doing so could possibly put her in jeopardy. Wait. Did I just say I'm falling *IN* love with her? How is this happening? Why can't I simply take this where I want it to go? Are we not physically compatible, or am I just shutting down again? I had been tainted by *something* that was out of my control, some beast who stole my choices and my freedom, and now this same *something* threatened a new chance at life and love. A dire sense of impending doom became part of a malicious cycle that would replay like a broken record, over and over, for the next five years of my life.

It was weird to be in that moment though, smoothing her shirt back down, trying to move forward. Exchanging awkward glances which revealed all the tracings of my vulnerability; and yet, there were no uncomfortable silences—everything went on the rest of the afternoon as it should. Jen's friend Shane and her husband at the time, picked us up and I scurried back home, sure that she would never speak to me again.

That night, the phone rang several hours later than my grandmother would have liked. I answered it with anticipation, only to hear Jen's voice on the other end of the line. My heart could finally stop plummeting into the pit of my stomach. And as I talked to her in the misty twilight, all I could think was *'Okay. We cool.'*

## Discovering the World Through Her Eyes

Over the next few months, Jen and I became inseparable. We also became insufferable drunks. I don't know if she ever knew it, but in all the time that I spent with her, I looked for every opportunity to hold her, touch her, kiss her, dance with her, just to be with her. These were the moments she may have been too drunk to remember, but I was too in love to forget. She taught me how to roll my tongue (nothing suggestive there...) She opened a world of literature and music to me that I had never known. I would go home with her favorite books in tow and spend endless hours reading classic rock stories such as *Wonderland Avenue*: a memoir about the life of Jim Morrison and The Doors, or *Pearl*: a chronicle of Janis Joplin's passions, addictions, and lovers.

We would stay up late into the night, listening to the entire discographies of Hole, Nirvana, and the Cure. I began to learn about who she was through music. We created our own language using song lyrics—a language that no one else but us could truly decipher. But that was ours, and always will be. Our secret world. So whether it was Courtney Love screeching *"I am the girl you know can't look you in the eye"* (Hole, *Miss World*) , or Robert Smith crying *"Whatever words I say, I will always love you"* (The Cure, *Lovesong*). Jen and I found our happiness in music, where our worlds would collide and at the same time—stand still.

She knew the perfect way to put a song into my soul. Her voice spun lyrics like silk, while her eyes placed them into me, woven into my very being. We stayed together in this surreal bliss for spiritual centuries. Somewhere in that space in time, I found the actual words to tell her I loved her. And in the magic of the night, she said it back. She always says it back. At some point in our relationship, we were pseudo "dating," but with her still being with Michelle, only her best friend Shane truly knew. Jen would later deny this, writing her story a little differently than mine. However, despite our status and her penchant for being the self-proclaimed "Queen of Mind Games," I knew for the first time in my life (far from the puppy love crushes of my past) what it felt like to be **IN** love.

Hanging by every word, being joined at the hip in everything we did or were, even having amazing phone sex with her, on several occasions—these are the things I remember. I remember a friend of hers, with the computer handle BFLO (because he was from Buffalo, NY) being on the phone during many of our conversations. She would run to grab a glass of water, and I would talk with him in intimate detail about how in love I was with her, what I wanted to do with her, to her; the body of the erotica novel that I had written exposed itself in the moonlight, as I read every tawdry detail, every echo from the truth of my heart. To this day, I question how much of these confessions Jen actually heard; whether she really left the room, or sat on the line, clinging to my every word. BFLO told me he liked me for her, more so than any other woman that she had had in her life. And he would encourage me. He continuously pushed me to let her know exactly how I felt. He would even work the conversation in my favor, pressing Jen for the answers I couldn't ask for and she could never truly answer, allowing me to profess my deepest desires under the guise of his questions rather than my needs. Aching, groaning, searching. Lust, I found, was part of the overwhelming feelings that were consuming me. As Janet Jackson once said in her famous song "Like a moth to a flame burned by the fire, my love is blind can't you see my desire?" (Janet Jackson, *That's the Way Love Goes*)

I shared everything with Jen. Everything except actual sex. The erotica novel I had written now emblazoned in my mind as a virtual road map to the types of experiences that I wanted to have with her. Every other sentence out of my mouth, for years on end, contained either the words "I love you" or some derivative of it. I crafted a mysterious and yet overt way of communicating with her. Gentle and yet aggressive. Sweet and sensual, with a tinge of dirt, like gravel grating into my mind, turning me, this innocent woman-virgin, into a voracious lover who wanted nothing more than to "fuck her brains out!" (Literally, my words!)

Every night would start and end with us. Soon, we began working together at Action Research, a telemarketing group that Jen already worked for and invited me to join, all to make sure that we limited our time apart. After work, after all the world was tucked away, here with each other we would remain. I melted every single time she spoke, with every strum of her Fender guitar, as I leaned against her bed, listening to our music, lost in her eyes. I stared at her for hours while she slept. This beautiful angel, passed out, FUBARED, and me, laid atop of couch cushions spread on the floor, because she hated people sleeping in her bed—*ME*, sleeping in her bed. Because then she was vulnerable, and all her efforts to push me away would fall apart.

She became mean at times, too much alcohol and all the unpredictable hormones in the air between us. Broken bottles and damaged doors. Holes in walls and screaming matches. After a while, she broke up with Michelle, but with our secret affair bordering the edge of a relationship already intact, she would never commit to what we actually were: together. Even to this very day. She was like a ship porting at different seas, always against my shore and yet off on new adventures at every turn. She pushed me away slowly, and I began to watch her fall again into yet another relationship, with Cheryl, this Celtic pagan girl from our workplace. This put me in the unsettling position of being the other woman for a second time. Being her unofficial girlfriend at the time that they hooked up broke my heart in two.

I know at some point our relationship changed to a mere friendship; maybe it always has been. I say that and yet, even to this day, I don't believe it. Not for one second; a breath or sigh in the vast naked wilderness of our love for one another. In the moments we shared, when she would say and do things a girlfriend does, those truths tell a different story.

I knew her darkest secrets. On the dark side, her mind games revealed a tendency towards hurting people. I trusted everything that came out of her mouth, laced with Exclamation! perfume and arsenic. What she would say to me in those tender moments when we were alone would be replaced with heartache when we were in the company of strangers. I would make a fool of myself, night after night, professing my love for her to the world, to her friends, and be rejected time and time again, unless it was just us, at the right moment. That's when it would turn magical. We would hold each other, whispering sweet nothings, looking into each other's eyes, and let the magic of our love sweep us away. *"Well, it's a marvelous night for a moondance, With the stars up above in your eyes"* (Jonathan Rhys Meyers "Moondace" from *August Rush*). It was in those midnight hours that I could truly call her more than a friend.

Even though she had her life and I had mine, when she finished her nights and came home, she would climb into bed, and before her head hit the pillow, we would be on the phone with each other again, without missing a single beat. There was even a time when she called me, right before losing her own woman-virginity, just to share that special moment of her life with me. Nervous and excited as she was, I talked her through it, sharing in her happiness, the whole time my heart crushed, wishing to be the one sharing those sheets with her. It was in this indefinable space between friends and lovers that I would hang my hat for years to come.

# A Series of Misadventures Among Misfits

There is a strange symbiosis that occurs while being in love with a best friend who is seemingly not in love with you. Even though your heart is continually breaking, the magnetism between you, especially in the unplanned moments, brings you together through what is emotionally the most difficult of circumstances. Being friends first, craving each other's company, being devoted to making sure that your time is shared with them, no matter what. Maybe on the off chance that this night will be different. That she will come to you and confirm all your deepest desires. That you can just sit in silence with her, and not talk about what you both know to be true. This, in turn, lent itself to some "crazy times at the school of hard knocks."

#TheHeartWantsWhatItWants

43

# Chapter 8

# Finding Me Within

## Tripping the Light Fantastic

One night while I popped some LSD that I copped from Denise—the same woman who deflowered Jen's female virginity—I experienced a life metamorphosis. It all started while at a sleep over with my friend Liz, who had been through a few trips before and wanted to take care of me during my first. As the night progressed, I suddenly experienced a separation from everyone when Liz fell asleep, and Jen and I, after having an unexpected round of phone sex, said our "goodnights" and "I love you's." I then felt compelled to take a long shower, surrounded with lavender. After stepping out of the bathtub, I sat down in front of the television and watched "The Wall" by Pink Floyd. As I drifted deeper into my daze, it slowly felt as if my heart stopped beating. The world went black and I sat there, suspended in the moment, until the next phase took hold. A few minutes later, I came to and walked into another room. I laid on the bed, staring between the heavenly lights of the ceiling fan and the evil darkness of an old black rocking horse in the corner. I chose to look up to the light of God and refuse the Devil's dark horse that night, as I masturbated all of the desires of my heart into the cosmos in the hopes that they would someday come true.

Minutes later, as I emerged outside on the lawn, I swam into an underwater utopian womb, lined with brilliant gemstones, and walked in a towel towards a sunrise on the riverbed, feeling as if I had been born again.

I would not find out until weeks later that I had been through an unintended but apparently fated religious indoctrination—discovering this in retrospect while on an impromptu reading adventure at Barnes and Nobles. As I researched multiple religious experiences, I came across *The Complete Guide to Witchcraft* by Raymond Buckland. *This was it! What I had experienced in the crystal haze of my own spiritual unfolding.* Just as in the five steps of Wiccan initiation outlined within the book, I too had gone through A Separation, A Ritual Cleansing, A Symbolic Death, A New Knowledge, and A Rebirth. The explanation fit my experience precisely; I had unknowingly and unintentionally via my LSD trip become self-initiated into the religious ways of Wicca.

Although I became well acquainted with Paganism, I never left my Christian roots. Whenever someone asked what religion I was, I would reply "I am Christian, Wiccan, Pagan, Shaman, Druid" because I believe that there are many branches to the same tree. Although I grappled with the issue of overlapping religions, as one's rules may sometimes negate the other, I understood more purely the purpose of all religion through my own unplanned initiation. Regardless of which branch I was on, I was walking a personal walk with my God, and even as an adult, that is something that few religious people ever truly do. I am not trying to make you believe **as** I believe, but merely showing you **what** I believe. I do not believe that a few hours a week of Church constitutes this walk. It's a walk that comes from deep within. It is a constant that comes from knowing that God created everything both in heaven and on earth, and through praising Him—respecting the fact that if we tap into just a few more percentage points of our usual brain's capabilities than we typically do, even if it happens to come about in drugs of enlightenment—that we can see this connection between religions as the outward manifestation of God. Our God is all these things because **God is Everything!**

# A Side Trip into Body Modification

A teenager bursting with enthusiasm and intellect, I found myself needing more physical stimulation and excitement and I knew the perfect way to accomplish this. A message to parents: One of the easiest ways to convince a teenager to make a spontaneous decision that goes against everything you wish for them is by forbidding them to do so. The second that my grandma said that I, now of the legal age of eighteen, could not pierce my tongue, I knew that it would happen. The only question was when.

On a random day, I walked down the twenty-minute route into the neighboring downtown village to pick up my paycheck and meet Jen for her break. When I arrived at our workplace, I ran into a coworker named Kevin. He was heading to a tattoo parlor to get his ears re-gauged, and I thought, *this is the perfect opportunity for me to get my tongue pierced*.

As we walked into the tattoo parlor, I heard the voice of my grandmother echoing in my head: "As long as you are under this roof, you will not be getting your tongue pierced." This, of course, was all the conviction I needed. However, my reasoning for the piercing was multi-faceted. First and most importantly, as a newly-emerging lesbian, I kissed a few select girls who had one. The pleasure I received from that was so wonderful that I wanted to be the one to make another woman feel that way, all soft and tingly inside. Also, I loved the fashion statement and thought that it was the perfect expression of my teenage angst. And lastly, it was my first true time asserting myself completely independent of my grandma's wishes. For all these reasons, I sat down with Chris, an expert piercer, and watched as he threaded cooled raw metal through the asymmetrical line highlighting the curvature of my tongue.

My first stop with my new jewelry was a small house party that Jen was at. I sat in the kitchen nursing a 40 ounce of St. Ides malt liquor, praying the impending pain from the piercing could be kept at bay. What I remember most is indulging in the fun of eating pasta with a tongue bar and the ritual of rinsing my mouth vigorously with Listerine, all in an effort to avoid infection while my self-inflicted wound healed.

Later that night, when we left the apartment, we headed across the street to a club called College Campus. This was one of my first introductions to the genre of breakbeat techno music. The bar hosted a DJ almost every night of the week, and even though it catered to a college crowd, it simply overlooked IDs. I remember being there with Jen, dancing, and watching her flirt with the new attractions of her life: a plethora of high school aged girls. Her soul mission in life then was to conquer the lot of them, and I came along for the ride. I even found myself attracted to one of them, Melissa, the most troubled, and ironically, the straightest of the bunch. On several occasions, Jen would end up topless, dancing on bar tables, running to the bathroom with me to outline her plans for the night, and whenever I could find the courage, I would kiss her. On this night, we would find ourselves fleeing the club while Jen's casual dating interest Maria was getting finger banged by three guys from the club. Jen and I would always find ourselves together, running from one adventure to the next, always right there for each other, getting into trouble and then finding our way out of dodge.

## Once In a Lifetime With Poppy Tears

On yet another fateful day, I showed up to the drug den that masqueraded as our job, just in time to see Jen walking towards our friend Tricia's cherry red V-8 Pontiac Firebird. As I went up to say hi, she tugged at my arm and muttered "get the fuck in." So I did. As I sat in the back seat behind the driver's side, I thought it would just be another day, smoking weed in the back of someone's car during their break. But what I got in return was beyond anything I could even imagine.

As Tricia packed the wooden bowl that Jen's girlfriend Denise had given her, I watched her sprinkle stardust over the herb and pass the pipe around, as Mountain's "Missippi Queen" blared through her speakers. And as I took a toke, the next thing—and the only thing I can remember—was the sensation of numbness that I felt when my head fell backwards of its own volition, onto the headrest made of clouds. And as I asked "what is it that you put on top?", Jen warmly replied, "baby, you're smoking opium".

## Astralling the World And Back

Even though we were on a permahigh and eternally out on the prowl, there were many nights where neither of us wanted to go anywhere. On another one of these endless phone-bound nights, I decided to put my newfound spiritual revelations to the test. For a while now, I had been experimenting with the depths of spiritual enlightenment—learning about candle magic and spiritual powers and the vast world that exists in the fields of meditation and astral projection. That, coupled with ESP (extra sensory perception) mind training exercises such as card reading telepathy, revealed that Jen and I's minds were in perfect sync. Our own mind reading games were registering results that would far surpass the psychological tests that I later found out were going on in labs around the world. On this magical night, I chose to play a new game, one of astral projection, which led me mentally into the room of Jen's newest infatuation, Quita.

As I brought myself to the right space and time to meditate, I concentrated enough to find my way to her home, to describe her walls and make something move from her desk; then I turned on her fan in the real world. As I came out of my trance, Jen received a frantic call from Quita. She was freaking out. In labored breath, she began to tell Jen about a strange terror that came over her. But when she mentioned her fan coming on and a loud sound in her room, my Jen knew I had truly been there.

And even though we were so close, there was a distance we could never overcome. I could feel her just beyond my reach, and on the tip of my lips, and yet not in my sex, though my loins ached constantly for her. For the most part, I left Jen to her playa ways and sat in the background, still hopelessly in love with her, but gaining a sick pleasure from watching her dominate the straight girls. She always wanted me there, sharing in her life, her loves, her being. However, during the times I could not be, I found myself in bed again with several people, faceless and nameless, or so you would think until you learn that I had documented them all in a not-so-little black book of my own.

## The Night I Blew it with the Bartender

It started at Last Call, a local after-hours B.Y.O.B. (bring your own bottle) club, with the bartender that I had been crushing on for a while. At the tender age of nineteen, I spent the entire night getting patrons to buy me drinks. As the club was closing at six a.m. in the morning, the bartender asked me if I wanted to come over and continue the party at her house. Excited at what the morning might have in store, and admittingly crushing on the bartender, I ended up going home with her, along with a guy nick-named Cosmos. We sat up drinking for a few more hours, Cosmos trying to get with me, and me trying to get with her. With both of our failed attempts, we drank until we were tapped out. I fell asleep with both bodies in the bed, completely innocent because we were all passed the fuck out. When we awoke, the three of us went down to the pool to sunbathe and somehow between my drunken stupor and my growing infatuation with this woman, I let it slip that I was only nineteen. She drove me home within the hour, and that was the last time I was allowed into that bar until I turned 21, ID in tow.

## My Crazy Attraction to Bartenders (Continued)

Did I mention Jen became a bartender? That, as her best friend and God only knows what else I was, I became privy to all the liquor my heart could desire? I would spend many years in an alcohol-induced haze as a direct result of this convenient fact.

During my early twenties, I spent countless nights at Memory Lane, the dive bar that she worked at, sitting on a stool towards the end of the bar. You could find me there almost any night of the given week, drinking ridiculously strong drinks, eating some of the best microwaved chicken wings that I have ever tasted, and piping money into the jukebox to listen to songs on repeat—all of which reminded me of Jen. Every moment that she could get away from behind the bar, we would find ourselves chain smoking with a beer in front of the pool tables. She taught me how to play pool like a pro, and I added my own geometrical understanding to this knowledge until I would go on to beat some of the most confident pool sharks in this town.

Meanwhile, during the times in which Jen was busy flirting with other women, like the bartender Ronda that we both had a crush on, I would simply find someone to take me home. Anyone. I could only put up with her confusion and rejection for so long until I found myself in the arms of yet another stranger. But in between the nights at the bar, and the endless nights in different beds, Jen and I found ourselves running around the entire county, hanging out with so many different people on different nights that I began to lose count of our social circles.

I mention this only to share with you just a few memories of those crazy nights; notably, some of the very few that I can still remember. Even on Jen's nights off from the bar, her being a bartender equaled us becoming hopeless lushes, in search of something. Maybe even each other.

## Where the Cool Kids Hang Out

This particular night started out like any other: Jen, myself, and some of the girls that we met through Action Research, ended up at a kegger under a bridge at the Merritt Island Causeway. This was not exactly our scene, but when the words "free beer" were involved, it quickly became ours for that night. Though the exact details are somewhat murky, I clearly remember the climax of the night. Jen, on a dare, ended up jumping into the river, and upon a subsequent dare from her, I joined in. We hung out and splashed each other like children, enjoying the water until we realized we could not get back up as easily as we had gotten down. Even though she could pull herself back out of the water, I had to swim around the entire underneath until I could find a spot to come back up on. So, as my partner in crime, she jumped right back in the water with me. Almost an hour later, as I wandered my way around the pillars beneath the bridge, I felt like a goddess, trying to impress the woman I loved. Although I was not very successful, as I kept slipping from the edges of not sturdy rocks and falling back into the recesses of the water, I tried nonetheless. My victory, much like that of life, ended up arriving from the journey more so than the destination. And as always, I stole a kiss from her for my accomplishment.

# The Dragon Tree

During my early twenties, Saturday nights held a certain reverence to me. Amidst the hectic nature of Jen and I's undefined relationship, there were many a night when I had to navigate my own world while she was busy playing in hers. Frequently I would do so with a glass of liquor in my hand and an endless sea of songs in my heart. But on this Saturday night, I spent the evening making love by candlelight to the *piano* in my room. I shut off the lights, closed out the world, and turned off the ringer to my phone. I opened the bedroom window and began to play for hours on end.

Throughout the night, many friends came to visit and to listen as I poured myself into those ivory keys. They would stay for a song and a drink and then proceed with their plans for the evening, each time, and I would make them leave without me. Again and again, they would try to convince me, begging me to go out with them, but I ignored each request. One after the other, I ignored each and every window caller... everyone except Jen.

***It was four in the morning*** and I couldn't mistake the growl of the green Ford Mustang outside my window. Even though my intentions were to stay in my room that entire night, I couldn't pull myself away from her. I just wasn't that strong. After all, the heart wants what it wants. There is no reasoning with it, no running away from it—no denying it. This was, however, a lesson that I would continue to learn even decades later, when I would return to this very feeling, when I would realize that she and I were inextricably linked by destiny.

But I digress...back to the dragon. Jen got out of her car, panicking and begging me to come with her over to her then-girlfriend Maria's house on the beachside. As she drove up to the edge of her driveway, Jen pointed at a tree in the distance. Sitting on the passenger side of the stang with a bottle of Malibu rum in a brown paper bag, we drove up as close as we could to the tree, and in the middle of the leaves, I could see a strange image or impression. It was the head of a dragon.

At first, I tried to reconcile myself to the fact that this was just the wind; that the shape and form that we were witnessing was merely an illusion that we both happened to conjure up, out of a not-so-drunken haze. But as we stared at the tree, we soon realized that this was clearly not the case. The body began to form, and as the dragon moved, it began shifting its gaze directly to us both.

We had discussed occult things numerous times before. We knew that Maria dabbled in some nasty devilish stuff, as had Jen in her earlier years, but the physical sensation of sheer terror and pervasive evil that enveloped us both let us know that it was not our collective imaginations. There was something about Maria in that dragon. It was evil and it was her. We stared at it for another moment or two, as I prayed for our safety. We left a few moments later. As Jen dropped me off at home, I felt like I had just witnessed death, reincarnated. This image played through my mind all night. Jen called me as soon as she got back home, and we discussed the evil tree before falling asleep with one another, as we always did, on the open phone line.

I always did everything I could to keep Jen safe. To keep us both safe. I expelled so much energy that night, and as we slipped into slumber, once again I knew beyond the shadow of a doubt that I had truly, for better or for worse, found my soulmate.

## The Saving Grace of Pride Rings

This was a night like any other. Jen and I on the phone till the wee hours of morning, laughing and loving each other and listening to music. On this occasion, however, my grandma was not having it. I must place a disclaimer here: although I love my grandma dearly, she was, after all, still human. She could still make decisions that I didn't agree with, and that is precisely what happened on the night in question.

Around three a.m., my grandmother, having had enough of Jen and I's conversation for the night, demanded that I hang up the phone. But when I outright refused, she resorted to physical measures: she pulled the phone out of the wall at the socket. I burst into the front room in a panic and shoved the phone back down onto the charger. However, in the midst of my ensuing verbal rage, the antenna on the top of the portable phone broke—its serrated metal edge cutting into my grandma's paper-thin skin. She, in turn, took this as the perfect opportunity to call the cops. In less than five minutes, a room full of patrolmen swarmed me, pushing me down with their knees in my neck, into our living room chair, and without asking for my version of the story at all, proceeded to handcuff me and hold me down aggressively, all while my grandma wove a sad tale about the granddaughter who was abusing her.

As I sat there listening in shock, I saw firsthand the extent of my grandmother's mean streak. Her vengeance at my late-night call was detailed explicitly to the cops in a story that teetered on the edge of outright lying, as she told them what a horrible granddaughter I was and how I tried to hurt her by cutting her with the antenna. They did not take this accusation lightly.

I was in serious trouble. With the mere thought of me committing elderly abuse, they were gonna lock me up and throw away the key for sure. As I thought about what it would be like to spend that night in jail, and thus became overcome with an extreme sense of terror and anxiety, my saving grace walked calmly into the room and came over to where I was handcuffed against the reclining chair.

She looked me dead in the eyes. In what seemed like hours of silence, she stared directly at my flannel shirt, and then she honed her eyes on the freedom rings around my neck.

Now, for those of you who do not know, the term "freedom rings" refers to a chain of metal rings that are the colors of the rainbow, which signifies belonging to the then-LGBT (lesbian, gay, bisexual, and transsexual) community. Freedom rings were a popular symbol of the "gay family" in the 1990s. After this female cop had assessed the situation and heard my proclamation that I was only 'on the phone with the girl that I was in love with', she promptly told the other officers to take the handcuffs off and leave because she would handle it. She then spent the next hour talking to both my grandmother and myself about my sexuality and how she believed that this was the true root of our whole problem. My grandma backed off of the abuse claim and the cop gave me a warm hug and told me it was going to be ok. (It always seems to end with an older woman hugging me and telling me it's going to be okay.)

I soon found that payphones, even in the middle of the night, were a much better choice for our marathon conversations than my home phone. Besides, being outside of the house gave me the freedom I needed to smoke cigarettes and drink alcohol and spend all my time, every waking moment, with this crazy girl whom I had fallen in love with.

## Pets, Pets, and More Pets

Then there was the night that I was walking while tripping on acid again, having snuck out my bedroom window after being invited to Jen's house, and walking twelve miles from my own, right to Jen's neighborhood. There, in the middle of the night, I stopped at yet another payphone. Listening to Melissa Etheridge's "Come to My Window" on the storefront radio drew me with desire to slip through Jen's window as I had done on so many occasions before. I was aching just to spend the night with her wrapped in my arms.

When I finally arrived within a block of her house, however, she couldn't let me come by anymore because her mom was screaming at her for being drunk, like always. She grounded Jen for her fucked up misadventures the previous night, in which a violent fight at our friend Tyra's party sent her running for her life to the inside of a closet.

Part of this night, however, was spent figuring out where in the hell it was that I walked to in the first place.

In a time before cell phones, it was our ritual, to sit up all night on the phone. I came up with a scheme along with Jen that would ensure our endless nights of conversation. I would merely go to a payphone, give Jen the number in the name message by calling collect, she would reject the call, and then I would have her call me back for free. This night, as I was walking in the shopping plaza right down the street from her house, I began tripping balls. And this is also the part where I got lost beyond belief. In the middle of a shopping wonderland, I was only able to identify the pet shop there, but I saw it go on forever. As I held the receiver in my morphing hands, I responded to her query for my location, "I'm at Pets, Pets, and More Pets..." because I saw a pet shop that went on forever, throughout the entire complex. All I could see was the pet store like an infinity mirror in my kaleidoscopic acid trip. We laughed for hours at my confusion, while the woman I loved laid less than a block away, curled up against her phone, and I continued pacing in anticipation of what would never be that night. What might never be.

## Cheating Death in a Little Red Sedan

And another day went by. As I pulled out of my driveway in my baby blue 89' Buick Skylark on a sunny afternoon, I anticipated the blast that I would have this night, just spending some quality time with Jen. It wasn't until I got to her house, however, that I discovered that Kirsty, an underage member of our friend group, would be hanging out with us as well. Did I mention she had just become an official runaway? I want to ensure I don't forget and leave that part out. It's kinda important.

Not knowing what to do but knowing that we couldn't stay at Jen's house, we hopped into Kirsty's car and made a beeline for the highway. But as we peeled out of Jen's driveway, we quickly became aware that we were not alone. Kirsty's brother had caught up to us in his car. He spent the next five minutes pressing up next to us with one of his friends and trying to box us in, while we swerved in and out of lanes, trying to get away.

Kirsty continued to speed up onto the freeway, in the process, she quickly attracted the attention of Brevard's finest. The radio blared Led Zeppelin's "Stairway to Heaven," as we attempted to evade both her brother, his friends, and the cops—then the trip started to take an even more dangerous turn. Watching the flashing red and blue lights in the rearview mirror, we zoomed past traffic, cranking up the radio to Don Mclean's "American Pie" and holding on tight to whatever we could grab inside the car. As the radio blared *"This will be the day that I die,"* Jen and I looked at each other, and, singing at the top of our lungs, we laughed nervously at the all-too-real 120 mph possibility that we, too, were going to die in that damn car. *"Bye bye Miss American Pie"*....

All in all, we sped back and forth to Orlando two times—a trip that would normally take about four hours. However, warping through traffic on the highway at such fast speeds, we completed the two round trips in less than one. We continued to fly up and down between lanes, taking sharp turns and unplanned exits back and forth, all the while failing to avoid the procession of concerned family members and law enforcement that were tracking our every move.

Eventually, we came back to US1, the car screaming through endless red lights and blasting through stop signs. As we were just coming around a bend next to the river and the nearby ice cream shop, we took a sharp and potentially deadly turn. We fish tailed off the edge of the road with the back tires and almost landed into the river water far below, a concrete light pole waiting for us in between. At this point, we had finally talked Kirsty into stopping because this had become way too dangerous, and as she pulled in behind an enclosed storefront, we thought we had lost the cops, until they surrounded the car thirty seconds later. We sat motionless, terrified of what was in store for us. Jen and I told the officers that we had no clue she was a runaway, and Kirsty told them she was going to kill herself, brilliantly setting the stage for the ultimate opportunity for all of us to get out of the daunting situation we had put ourselves in.

At this point, the officers actually told us that they were going to let the chase go if we had not pulled over, because had we crossed into the next county, they would have considered it too dangerous to continue the pursuit. Either way, we were incredibly lucky that day. The cops carted Kirsty off to Circles of Care, a psychiatric facility where she would be under suicide watch for seventy-two hours, and after the cops let us go, we walked over to the ice cream stand and used a payphone, our favorite thing, to call Jen's mom to come get us the hell outta there.

As we drove home, it became abundantly clear in our minds that this was our first run-in with serious trouble. We could have just as easily ended up in jail that night.

It became part of our M.O to get out of numerous situations that could have been jailable offenses. I believe we may have even made a name for ourselves around town with the police department. Two relatively good kids who seemed to always get themselves into trouble, but who were respectful to the police and, if the cops did any digging, they would come to find that we were also very dedicated to our respective home lives. At this point, I was taking care of my grandma on a more regular basis, and Jen was, as she had always been, a family person as well. All I knew was that being around each other, we seemed to be invincible. And in the long nights ahead when we would continue to tempt fate by drinking outrageous amounts of alcohol and driving all around hell's creation, that bond that we were continuing to build just grew stronger with every passing day.

## Yet Another Time That We Should Have Been Arrested

While writing, I find myself vacillating between the 'then' and the 'now'. While writing this autobiography, I woke up a few days ago to this current-day text:

**Jen:** "Good morning my little ray of sunshine. Here's a chapter for your book. I was getting on the elevator at work to go home and I remembered a night where just me and you went to Orlando, downtown in your car, and we were blasting techno and you were having fits in the front seat. You were blowing up on ecstasy, punching the dashboard and being a freak, and I remembered that the cops pulled up next to us at the stoplight and told you to stop it. Stop it! LMFAO!!!!! Remember that!"

Our brushes with law enforcement, it seemed, were inevitable and continuous. Even in the moments that I can no longer remember due to endless nights of drinking and drugging, Jen will not let me forget our good times. And she will never ever let me forget the beauty of our life together. A life that we chose to live as partners a long time ago.

## Three Girls, Two Beers, and A Boat

As the years went by, Jen and I got closer and closer, and the world got further and further away from us. Like any typical night, Jen, Shane, and I drove down to the river to do what we always did best: get drunk. As we pulled up in our little hidden cove this time, I was dismayed to see that there was a "No Parking" sign where we had always parked before. 'This won't do,' I thought to myself. Seeing that the sign was leaning a little bit out of its foundation, I knocked it down and pulled it out of the ground, taking my trophy with me down to the river, hidden from the prying eyes of Florida's finest.

While we basked in the breathtaking scene of the river in moonlight, Jen and I saw a beautifully dilapidated wooden boat and decided to borrow it without permission and take a short adventure into the middle of the river together. Shane bowed out of the experience, which left Jen and I, stupid and stricken, to jump into the boat's raggedy core and make our way up stream with only the sign as a paddle. As we pushed hard through slightly choppy waters, trying ever so delicately not to tip the boat over, we turned on a portable radio and settled into our mission, and our arms battled the water when the signpost slid into the river abyss as we defiantly fought the urge to rush back to safe shores.

Flailing our arms as makeshift oars now, we quickly came to the realization that we were about half a mile out to sea. So we rested in the river for a moment, listening to the radio as Alice Deejay's "Better Off Alone" spoke in our silences, and Jen and I drifted with the push and pull of the tide.

After returning the boat to a separate place in the middle of the river rather than the place in which we took it from, we slammed our beers and headed towards land. It was then that I saw a buoy bobbing up and down in the water and wanted a small memento from the night, so I grabbed ahold of its top and drug it towards the shore. Little did I know, as we abandoned the boat to swim to land, that I was hauling a full-size crab trap in tow. Each stroke towards the sand became more difficult, weightier. At some point, we all had to carry the damn thing to get it into the car. But I was persistent. I wanted the medal to go with the memory; one that has now stuck with me throughout all time, as an amazing bonding adventure of the two rebellious lovers in their midnight interludes.

A tip to all of you crabbing enthusiasts: blue crabs from the Indian River are not appetizing...*AT ALL!* I remember coming home to Jen's house that night, drunk as a skunk, and begging her mom to prepare them while I stood there, dumbfounded. It turns out that it really is the journey, rather than the destination, that ends up having the most significance in my life. The crabs tasted awful!

All at once, towards the end of the evening, the boat truly became a metaphor for something else as well. It was a confined space in which both Jen and I were navigating uncharted waters, trying to figure out our place in them. And even to this day, we still are.

## With The Good, Comes the Bad...

It's easy to write about the good times. What is not easy, however, is wording the bad ones in a way that people don't judge, they simply listen. Being able to tell the difference between what you would do—and what I actually *did* do—is the key. Just know that, in everything, love was the aim; it is, after all, the highest goal that we can ever strive for. As Eden Ahbez once put it "The greatest thing you'll ever learn is just to love and be loved in return" (*Moulin Rouge*).

Jen and I went through an amazing amount of loving moments, but we also were the self-perpetuating victims of a ridiculous amount of personal dramas. She threw me out of a moving car once while I was drunk and belligerent. She left me at a party where I would end up being sexually assaulted for the second time in my life. She pushed my heart away, telling me that she was not into me like I was into her. She told me she was not physically attracted to me, killing any chance of a real relationship, and yet pulled at my heart with a genuine love and affection that kept me hanging on. She had shown her hand as shallow, not seeing a woman from the inside out but from the outside, in. What she never understood was that she could have looked anyway at all, and my heart would still feel what it felt. What it still feels. For her.

Once, I got mad at one of my old junior high friends, Nancy, for trying to hook up with Jen, knowing full well just how much in love with her I was. As a close friend, I had confided my love for Jen to Nancy on several occasions. Even though she would tell me how I didn't need her, how I could find so much better, I would still lose my front tooth in a brawl with her, over her overtly flirtatious advances. I knew that she was more into trying to sleep with Jen than being a friend to me when, after I began freaking out while Jen and her were making out, Nancy slammed my face against a refrigerator and knocked out my front tooth. Meanwhile, Jen just sat on and watched, and laughed...and did very little else.

# The Path of Self Destruction

One of the best ways to get over one woman is to crawl up under another. This is exactly what I was attempting to do when, out of the blue, I met Lori—the no-name girl who would put my life in jeopardy while I tried to get over my broken heart.

Somewhere in my early twenties, I found myself striving to move away from Jen for a while, just to have a chance to have another relationship. I was unable to handle hanging out with her as much after the trauma of my busted face, knowing that while everyone was trying to hit that, I just wanted her in my life, my space, my world. And I didn't want their trifling asses near her. But I couldn't handle Jen's rejections, night after night, that would tear my self-worth and my dignity apart. Instead, I somehow found myself hanging out with a girl I hardly knew, all the while taking a mental inventory of my feelings over Jen. This led up to me hanging out with people

I didn't know, on the off chance that I would be able to stand being away from the woman my heart knew all too well.

On this fateful night, I was divinely saved from a bad decision just in the nick of time—too messed up to get myself out of it, and in the end, lucky to still have my life. How I met the girl doesn't matter. Only the events that led up to my first diagnosed psychosis. It all went down like this:

I was driving with this new "friend" Lori when we came upon two good-looking boys whose truck had broken down on the side of the road. Being the sucker that I am, I stopped the car to see if they needed help. Meanwhile, I had been trying to hook up with Lori all night. She, on the other hand, proceeded in trying to hook us both up with the two guys. After giving their truck a jump, the two boys rewarded us with some purple mescaline gel tabs and then they invited us to come over the next night to a party off Aurora Road and drop the gels with them.

*I should preface this: People always tell you when you are using drugs, that you will either end up dead or in a ditch. The latter is exactly what happened to me.*

I had just shown up to the stupid party where I didn't know anyone because Jen was busy with all the little high school girls that night, and I was just trying to get laid. I walked in, feeling like I knew exactly what I was doing, hoping to run into the girl I had been trying to hook up with all weekend. As I walked through the front room and into the kitchen, Lori was just walking out with some guy. We bumped into each other and she said she would call me tomorrow. So, I found myself alone, again, and had nowhere else to go. Instead of returning home, which would have been the smart thing to do, I found myself staying at the party and dropping two of the gel tabs that were still in my car's center console. I was living in the delusion that I would be safe. That this party would be like a surreal dream, me hallucinating in black lights and dancing with loud music blaring all around me. About thirty minutes later, however, the gels had still not kicked in, so I sat down on the couch, waiting for my adventure to begin. I remember a guy sitting with a gun on the table next to me and telling me to take the Darvocet that sat in a bottle next to it. I felt trapped, so I did as he said, and I washed it down with a beer. The next thing I remember of what happened came straight out of a nightmare.

It was about an hour or so later. At this point, the gels were just starting to hit my system—their potency mixed with the alcohol and pills I had already ingested. Soon after, I proceeded to get so fucked up, that I found myself being groped in a three-way make out session teetering on the edge of madness, as strange people I did not even know were ripping and pulling at my clothes. When I finally came completely to, a lady and her boyfriend were gnawing at my body, trying to throw me down onto the bed. They became quite violent, grabbing and clawing at me like vicious animals.

Freaked out and unable to remember how I got there, I slipped away from them and ran out the back door. And that is when the gel tabs kicked in. Running away from them through a seemingly simple enough backyard turned into a flashback of running away from the Viet Cong in a jungle of thick brush. I could feel my body moving in slow motion; rubbery, and my eyes flashed with color, as I ran terrified through the neighboring backyards. When I finally made it through the woods, I hopped into my car, and against all better judgment, I started driving toward the singular red light which appeared as four lights in my impaired vision.

I had almost made it to the main road, until I felt I was going to pass out. I needed to rest, and so I pulled up next to a garbage dumpster at a local convenience store parking lot to just sleep it off. But as I was made aware by the store employee tapping on my window that I had double-parked, I quickly attempted to drive forward and around to get into a better spot. Unfortunately, I pressed reverse, and instead of moving forward, landed myself straight backwards into a ditch.

When the cops came, I knew I was in major trouble. I was driving intoxicated and had no real clue where I was. I also knew I had been assaulted in some way by those people, but I didn't know to what extent, or if I had been a willing participant until I came out of my blackout. As I explained this to the very angry officers, their mood changed. The cop cars were replaced by ambulances, and I was on the way to Holmes Regional with an IV of Thorazine, a drug that they give to people who have overdosed on LSD.

# Bad Trips and Plane Crashes

After arriving at the hospital, I do not remember the first few hours. As I came out of the glossy daze, my grandmother was sitting in a chair next to my hospital bed, and I was just starting to realize how much trouble I was really in.

Luckily, the police had dropped the taking-me-to-jail routine, as it was replaced by the leering glances of the medical staff which was not sure whether I was just making everything up, or if I had been attacked. That made two of us. In the future, I never counted that moment as an assault, because I do not know whether I was so high that I consented or not. I don't even remember how far we all went. All I know is that I felt unsafe at some point in the night, and that is when I ran for my life.

I was released to my grandmother's care the next morning. As I got home and in bed, I remember that she tried to serve me pancakes and orange juice. I refused. Food was unbearable. After twelve more hours of not coming down, I told my grandmother I was really scared, and she drove me back to the hospital. This is when the ambulance came to take me from there to Circles of Care. I had been Baker Acted.

Note: If you are a danger to yourself or others, the state can step in and put you under surveillance at a mental hospital. This is what happened to me. Welcome to the Baker Act.

I arrived at the institution unsure of why I was there. When they asked for my name, I remember that I panicked and wrote 'Garfield'. As I walked through the corridor leading to the main room, I saw a news broadcast flash across the screen. There had been a horrible plane crash, and there were no survivors. All at once I felt this immense sense of horror wash over me as I began to believe that I was dead from that same crash and that this was my own personal hell.

It took several packs of cigarettes and plenty of bedrest to get me back to some semblance of normality. I spent everyday pining for Jen, but was too ashamed to call her to tell her what I had done, where I was. All I needed was to see her face. Instead, I would see the faces of our mutual friends Price and

Jackie on visiting day, but not as my visiting friends. They were also in the mental institution that weekend. I always wondered if they got a hold of the same bad batch of gels that I did—the ones that took my life symbolically in a blaze of fire.

But this would not be the last time that I shut Jen out. After crying myself to sleep while she participated in an orgy on Linda's floor, I found myself needing more and more space away from her. Not only could I not take the debauchery, but I was seriously hurting because all I ever wanted was to be there in her arms listening to music like we would before, while the whole world simply went away. But she was off making plans and sleeping around, never knowing how much it killed me inside to see her like that. To see her as my sometimes-never lover.

I even spent time in the arms of an abusive man, pushing cocaine poison into my veins so that I couldn't feel her running through them. Even though she was not nice to me during this time, calling me every explicative in creation, telling me what an asshole I was for being with him, Jen understood. I think she just knew how real, how unconditional my love for her was, and that I was only with him because I couldn't be with her. Maybe that scared her, or maybe she found it endearing. Maybe there was even a space in time where she held the same feelings for me. I guess I will never know for sure. All I know is that, when years later my girlfriend of two and a half years left me for another woman in a threesome gone horribly wrong, Jen spent the night with me. Tears filling my eyes, she looked at me with the softness of an angel, danced with me slowly around her room to Wham's "Careless Whisper", and then, taking my head into both her hands, kissed me in the gentlest and most heartfelt kiss I have ever felt, or will ever feel again. Suspended in that moment (because as I would one day tell her "all we have in *life* are *moments*"), she told me that she would do "anything to make me feel better, just name it." I wanted desperately to whisper *make love to me* in her ear, as I rested my head against her shoulders. My answer? "Just hold me, until this pain goes away." And, as I laid wrapped in the strength and security of her arms, that is exactly what she did.

#TheHeartWantsWhatItWants

# Chapter 9

## Battling with Demons

### The Darkside:
### Living Through Human Trafficking

This is the hardest thing I have ever had to write. It is not until now, in my late thirties, that I have even truly seen this past period of my life for what it was. I was in love with Jen, I was hanging out with her old-time junior high school friends, and I was a victim of human trafficking.

Back then, it wasn't looked at quite like that. It didn't have a flashy name: I was an innocent kid who just wanted to get to know everyone Jen knew because maybe it would bring me closer to her. That's when I decided to start hanging out with one of her childhood friends. She was the first woman to ever kiss Jen, and this made her especially important in my never-ending quest to understand just what made Jen tick.

*I will note here that this woman is no longer with us. She went through a battle with her own personal demons; one that she lost. Everything that I say in this section needs to be tempered with this one fact: I have forgiven her for her transgressions against me, and I pray that she finds peace wherever she is now, in the great beyond.*

While Jen gallivanted along with several of the straight girl crew, I spent my time hanging out with her old friends. I'll give Jen the credit that she said her friends were bad news, but that didn't stop me from wanting to know them in any way possible. I mean, after all, association is assimilation.

Jen's friends were also into heavy drugs. I drove them around on several occasions, while they would shoot up in my car. I remember one time in a parking lot where one of the friend's family members nodded out on the side of my car after shooting Dilaudid, a synthetic opioid, into her and her boyfriend's veins. This would be the same drug that I would later take with that same woman and my pseudo-boyfriend Matthew, as we skirted the edge of a dangerous game.

This is so hard to write, it will all come out fragmented, because it fragmented me. One time, I was at a house with Jen's friend in West Palm Beach and she wanted to do my makeup. She made me look like a china doll. I thought, back then, that it was cute. It was girls being girls, doing makeup, and I didn't know how to do it myself, so I went with it. She told me I was beautiful and that she really wished Jen and I would go be with men instead of women because it wasn't natural what we were doing. And I went along with it, just like when she kissed me because she wanted to know "what that feels like '", what "Jen had felt," as she said. Just like I went with the guy that she would "hook me up with" later that night. And even years later, I only vaguely put two and two together. She was using me as an escort for her male clients and had me all made up like a girly-girl to get money or drugs from pawning me off on men. She said she was setting me up on dates. I was heartbroken that Jen didn't want to be with me officially, so I rebelled in any way that I could.

So I went on dates with men. And they always ended the same way. Every time I slept with a guy on top of some parked car, or gave him a hand job in the woodlands, or went out with someone like Matthew who was a complete drug addict, or Peter who actually ended up being a close friend and lover—albeit a married one—it tore me further away from Jen and brought me down a path of sexual torture. I can only now see this fact clearly, as a current teacher who has been through many years of professional development sessions about human trafficking—all of which were designed to help us recognize this crime so that we could help our students avoid it. But in this case, acknowledging it has made me relive it from my own past. It isn't always the horrible scenario of the international human trade with girls shackled, wasting away on a bed or an 18-wheeler full of beaten up and drugged girls. Sometimes it's just a drug addict; some pills, some cash, and an easy mark—Me.

## The Church's Denial of Lesbians: A Debate with the Pastor

Although I had now lived through some of earth's craziest hells, I still held on firmly to my belief in God.

*I preface this section with a simple statement of purpose: it is not written here for me to preach religion to someone, but rather to show the unending struggles that I have experienced personally as a Christian homosexual.*

First, let's review the facts: I grew up with my grandma in a Christian Presbyterian family. I played piano for our home church, *Sebastian by the Sea*; as a child, I attended Christian school; as a teen, I taught children to play piano and became a musical accompanist to a church choir; and in my early twenties, I played Christian hymnals for my grandma and made my first attempt at reading the entire Bible. My heart has been filled with the Lord's good word and grace since I could remember. And yet, in the times when I truly needed Him the most, I would find that the social doors to his love were closed off for people like me, if I were to be honest about who I really was. If I was to love women.

One of the hardest life struggles that faces a young homosexual is keeping and expressing their connection to God. Even when I held unconditional love for God in my heart, it would become painfully apparent in my adult life that God's people did not always have unconditional love for me. The knowledge that you could be judged and hated simply for loving someone just didn't make sense to me. What did make sense, however, was to experience the love of God in any way that I still could.

During one particularly beautiful music program at a local Church in Florida, I felt the presence of God seep into my very skin. The energy in the room was penetrating; while hugging your fellow brethren, you could feel a human quality of love and goodness; an acceptance of your fellow man, or so I perceived. As the special guest Gospel singer concluded their praise song, I instantly saw a glorious light beam emanate from his head into the very heavens above. I felt ecclesiastically pure and whole in this moment and wanted to know how I could become a member of this church. Excited to have found a new potential church home, I set up an appointment with the pastor for the next week, and joyously awaited the moment that I could call this new church my new church family.

As I walked through the hallowed doors to the pastor's counseling room, I knew that in order to feel like I was truly one with the church, I would have to disclose everything about me, including my sexuality. I started by expressing the love that I have in my heart for God, and the things that I have done in my life for His glory. Then, as a sidebar, I confided that me and my girlfriend were both interested in joining the parishioners. At once, like the turning-off of a light, I saw the pastor's demeanor change. This man sitting across from me went from being an advocate of God to a single judge, jury, and executioner of my calling to be a part of his congregation.

"Well, you are welcome to come to church services, but we do not allow homosexuals to become members," he replied.

I was confused. Wasn't this exactly what a Christian church strove for? To have the message of God reach as many people as possible? **To "love thy neighbor as thyself?" (Mark 12:31).** I knew I needed to voice my opinion.

"I understand that you look at my sexuality as a sin. What I don't understand is how, if everyone is born into original sin, you can look at what you perceive as mine and deny me the ability to come into a family whose very point is to work towards a closer relationship to God, and to help repent for sin."

I continued to plead my case by citing the very scriptures that have caused this divide between the homosexual community and the church. **"In Leviticus 18:22, it says [as a man] 'thou shall not lie with mankind;**

**it is an abomination.'** But I feel that this was written many years ago when people were not in loving homosexual relationships but were giving God the finger by doing perverse sexual things, as an actual spiting of God. They were blatantly acting on a hatred of God rather than the love that He put in their heart. The same love that I have shared with my monogamous girl-friend for the past two years."

He replied. "That may be so, but the church simply will not allow it."

I spent the next twenty minutes explaining that I do not love women because I hate God, I love women because God made them and made me this way. I told him that I knew the scripture rather well and had searched in my heart for quite a while before coming out, but still he held the church doors closed. At the end of our time together, however, he told me one final thing that truly made me see the church as the ultimate hypocrisy:

*"I AGREE with you. But I can't allow you to become a member. I will send you some literature from the church, though, to express our position."*

Not to my surprise, that literature would never come. I would then spend several years of my life feeling that I was unworthy of God's love. Even though I prayed and wrote in a praise journal every day, I always felt like I was walking a solitary path with God that the church condemned.

I struggled with the general existential questions of humankind's existence, the battle over one's own sin, just like most faith-driven humans do, but what has been different is that, for what was seen as MY sin, it was game over. Almost all other sins can be forgiven, even those which break the Ten Commandments, however, the one that I was seen as committing through holding a different interpretation of Bible scripture (for there are only about seven verses throughout both the Old and New Testaments of the Bible which directly address homosexuality as being wrong); this was unforgivable. I was damned to hell simply for being alive and being honest about who I love.

# Judge Lest Ye Be Judged

Another challenge growing up gay came from within the community itself. It wasn't enough that Christian spiritual leaders considered me a sinful pariah, but the very leaders of the community that were there to help me along my journey into adulthood treated me like an outcast. Well, that is partially true. In most cases, I was seen as an anomaly in a continuous wheel of failed assumptions and lacking diagnoses. I confused all of them because I broke the mold. Let me explain.

I'll start with the "ther-*rapists*," as they were lovingly termed in the movie *Girl Interrupted*; this category includes a group of individuals which I sought intermittently throughout different stages of my life when, just like most well-adjusted *heterosexual* people, I—as a lesbian, also needed some psychological guidance. When I mentioned in passing that I was a lesbian, not coming to them with "lesbian problems," but with *human* problems, most of them delved right into the Freudian "homosexuality questions," a term I have affectionately coined in which all mental health professionals run through a grocery list of possible explanations for your "gayness." It always goes the same way:

**One:** *Have you ever been with a man sexually?* ("Yes? Okay! There's still hope...")

**Two:** *Have you ever been sexually abused?* ("Yes. Okay, that might be it! I mean, why you went to women...")

**Three:** *Do you have any strong male role models in your life?* ("No? Raised by your grandma? Check! That could be it... I'm getting warmer...")

**Four:** *When did you first realize that you were gay?* ("Wait a minute... you didn't know the term "gay," because you were sheltered... I get that, but you've felt this way since childhood? Well, that changes things... Excuse me for a second... I can't seem to find a place to mark this on the matrix") and on and on and on. It was as if I was not there for normal life concerns or just simple counseling. In fact, every psychologist had to get to the bottom of this whole gay thing—the thing that must be the source of all of my troubles. But, what they were not expecting, is to all come to the same conclusion, even, in some instances, after several months of counseling.

Scene: Enter the Dr. with a notepad, a pen, and a tape recorder. He or she sits down in their leather desk chair, crossing their legs at the knees, and passively chews the bottom of their pen before inking and recording these words:

*"Regarding patient X: Overall, the patient is well adjusted. She seems rather smart and optimistic about life, she is very caring and kind, actually quite altruistic, and she does not seem to have any mental abnormalities other than her own insecurities. No recommendations for treatment or referral to psychiatric evaluation are required at this time."*

Imagine that! And as far as being insecure about society? Very odd indeed, especially for such a well-adjusted lesbian.

As if the psychologists' preconceptions were not enough, then we move onto the Professors of my college years. One professor in particular: Dr. Alfonso, pushed the envelope even further when he declared all gay people as child predators. Week after week, I would sit and listen to this man who held a Doctorate in Education, drone on and on about how gay people have a hidden agenda to both abuse and convert children into being gay. He would go on to explain that they then protect each other from high positions in the educational field, creating a cone of silence around the sexual abuse of children. To be lumped into a group of child molesters made my blood boil and my skin twinge. Here I was, just beginning a career in teaching, and this man was programming me to believe that I was a monster, simply because of my existence.

While most of my gay brothers and sisters stood up to this constant bullying, I kept rather quiet. I even became his teacher aide and went with him on several field trips with the local school children. I received an A plus in his course, as he continuously told me how much good I would do for the teaching community, all the while abandoning, and thus silencing, my homosexual family AND, for the first time in my life, myself. I took the lower road by not standing up for myself and the homosexual community. In essence, I allowed the social injustice against gay people to continue. Later in life, I would pay for this choice dearly, when I would begin to question, and at times abhor, my very own homosexual nature simply because of these wonderful professionals that helped shape me into a needlessly neurotic and hopelessly worrisome lesbian, who was almost programmed to believe that all homosexuals molest children.

## Whatever it Takes to Get You Through The Night

While I continued my spiritual quest for God's acceptance and my social quest for the acceptance of my peers, I took many exciting but dark turns. In the process of living my life and letting Jen live hers, I experienced a million nights of restlessness, searching for the one thing that could help me move past her. I looked in the recesses of friends, lovers, drugs, sex, and music for the answer to an impossible puzzle. *How do I fit in the world if I am not with her; when she IS my world*?

I started to branch out more when, after not showing up for a shift that I didn't even know I was scheduled for, I was fired from Action Research. I then became a telemarketer for DIRECTV, at an installation store directly behind my apartment complex.

As an aside to young aspiring adults seeking a job: I earned my position by being relentless and showing up every day for a week to a job I had not yet been hired for. By the end of the week, the owner was so impressed with my dedication that he put me on the schedule, and I quickly moved up the ladder. I went from an entry level employee position to becoming the General Manager of the entire company, and secretary to the owner as well, in less than a year.

During this time, I also became the hiring boss for many people. These would soon become close personal friends of mine. I remember one friend, Joey, the gay boy who became my best friend, if only but for a brief moment in time. I would spend every weekend with him, throwing our version of "pharm" parties, in a tiny one-bedroom apartment, just east of downtown. The entry fee to one of our soirees was either some type of drug or booze. Every night we would sift the ecstasy pills from the pile to take for ourselves, and then leave the remainder of various party favors for the party goers. I would then proceed to play Rick West's *Flavored Beats 4* in its entirety, and on repeat, but not one person complained. By the end of the night, Joey would retire to his room to get head from a random stranger, and I would proceed to hit on several women, making their conquest my nightly endgame.

Meanwhile, I also worked sixteen-hour days at my job, eventually turning my employees into my dating pool. One of my fellow supervisors in particular, Melinda, claimed profusely that she was straight but that there was "just something about me" that she simply couldn't resist. We would, inevitably, hook up several times during the next few years. I even found myself in bed once with both her and Tom, a close friend whom she claimed was dying of cancer, during a weekend of threesome sex in which I helped him knock a special goal off his bucket list.

Then there was Joey's downstairs neighbor Rachel, a fun-loving girl who was experimenting with bisexuality, and I was her latest science project. We began our brief fling with two glasses of red wine and ended it with her mental institutionalization. This was the extent of my drug-induced haze with Joey. It would be followed seemingly endlessly by countless other nights with random strangers, trying to escape the pain of a love that I still felt; a love that might just be eternally unrequited.

## On with the Show

I do not want you to think that I simply sat back and obsessed after Jen, brooding in a dark room somewhere on the edge of insanity. There were those dark times—in bed, in tears, on the verge of contemplated suicide, but before I knew it, my life took a different and dynamic direction. In addition to my new career as a General Manager, I began playing piano weekly at a nearby coffee shop; in addition to random gigs around town,

I was slowly building a small name for myself as a local musical artist. I would later be offered a few big breaks gone by: a recording contract with a Christian label, which I had to turn down for some pretty-obvious reasons, a chance to join Secondhand Serenade after a concert at the Knitting Factory, which fell apart after the lead singer John's Capitol Records label decided to keep him as a solo artist, and an offer to become a songwriter for Keyshia Cole, which I let slip through my fingers. I also had mind-blowing sex with numerous multi-gendered partners, wonderful relationships with a few amazing women, and eventually, I fell in love again. It is only that, throughout it all, Jen was there with me. She was the fixed gear in a world full of moving pieces. Somewhere deep inside my soul, my *heartlight* still burned for her.

## Play On, Playa

Since Jen had become so good at being a player, I thought I would try my hand at the game. I then proceeded to spend several evenings with other countless strangers, getting by...by getting high. I remember one night at the Treehouse, a local dive bar, in which I achieved my own self-proclaimed lesbian goddess status when I slept with a sexy ass slutty bartender. After a long night of small club raving, a tradition that had taken over many ordinary bars around Brevard County (more about that later), I found myself wrapped in the arms of Erica, yet another stranger that I seduced with my own game. A hot ass stranger! All I can remember is that, while rolling incessantly, hours after the DJ's record needle had screeched to a halt, I was listening to some late-night techno on the jukebox. That's when Erica pushed me onto the barstool and began to give me a lap dance. For me, it has almost always started with a lap dance or a brush against a bathroom wall.

As she weaved her seductive powers around my body, I built up my nerve to kiss her, and, in the heat of the moment, we ended up on the pool table. She laid me down against it, pulling my "Shut the Fuck Up and Dance" t-shirt off, and my baggie JNCO khakis, while the male bartender, who was also her boyfriend, watched on, and later joined in.

This was not my last one-night stand by far. Throughout the next few years, I would share the bed of many women, on many an occasion, sometimes even completely unintentionally. One of those such nights that stands out in my mind is the time when I slept with Corinne as the result of a simple bet. We were just hanging out, walking downstairs at my apartment, when we found a massive satellite dish: a dinosaur relic from circa 1990, a time in which these metal behemoths were roughly the size of a small car. That was when this seemingly straight woman posed a challenge to me during my drunken stupor; one that I undertook more so on principle of the challenge than on my own attraction to her, which in reality, didn't even exist.

Inspired by both my wild spirit and my desire to make women happy, Corrine made her move. "If you can lift this dish up the stairs to my apartment, I will fuck you." My eyes lit up like saucers at such a butch request. Challenge accepted. Showing off my lesbian bravado, I manhandled that satellite like a boss, working it up one stair after the other, albeit slowly. Every two or three steps though, the dish slipped down to the stair before. However, I was able to get it up the first flight before my strength dissipated completely. In a cruel twist of irony, and to make matters worse, Corrine just happened to live on the second floor. 'Great.' I thought to myself.

'How am I ever going to get this thing up *there*!'

I would later find that my very attempt to do this for her was a major turn-on. Corrine, after laughing for a few minutes at my futile determination, finally gave in. Grabbing the other end of the satellite dish with me, she helped me walk it up the second flight of stairs. When we reached the top, we both started kissing, and the satellite dish went careening back down the staircase. But this did not deter us. We merely laughed at the sight of this huge dish crashing to the ground and proceeded to walk into our friend Tracy's house and take over her bedroom. As TLC's "Kick Your Game" came on, we laid down together at dusk and didn't finish until dawn. The next day, with sore muscles and the good kind of body aches, we went to a makeshift carnival. Corrine won a cute little stuffed panda for me to commemorate our time together, and this was the end of our midnight tryst.

During this time of sexual adventure, I also found that I was not completely against being with men, all in an effort to be with women. I casually dated quite a few guys in the process of fucking women. I can remember one night, when my boyfriend Wayne and I went into a strip club and picked up a blonde stripper named Kim. We proceeded to do cocaine with her throughout the entire morning—a dragon that quickly became my drug of choice. All I remember of that night is the expensive white walled apartment that she lived in and the three of us waking up in bed together in the late morning after a night of loveless sex.

## A Quick Lesson in Easy Money

While we are on the subject of strippers, here's a nice tip. If, as a woman, you ever want to earn money at a strip club without shedding a thread of clothing, follow this simple rule: kiss a stripper.

The night started with a trip to see Starr at work. Just an innocent trip, partly out of boredom, to see a new friend. Being somewhat attracted to each other, we kissed for a minute, flirty with each other, me a patron of the club; her a stripper, and without even offering a dance, men began to throw money at the both of us. Once we realized how much money could be made from our seemingly unplanned attraction, we continued kissing and touching throughout the night. The money poured in. The men didn't even need lap dances. They would just watch us together and pay! We spent many a night running this scam, buying drugs with our profits and getting fucked up to oblivion on a nightly basis. I would find out later that this very woman was related to Jen's aforementioned friend, and I would also end up rolling around on bedsheets with her and Matthew, on the night before they asked me to run away to New York with them.

I waited patiently at the house while Matthew booked our plane tickets. But when evening came, and he stopped by to see if I was ready to go, I reluctantly told him no. Something told me not to go.

*Newspaper Headline: Matthew and Starr were arrested the next week after committing a bank heist in New York.*

These types of crazy nights blurred in my mind as Jen ran off with a myriad of women, looking to take each of their female virginities. I spoke to her after almost every conquest, almost every night, but we would also take time apart, engaged in mutually separate one-night stands.

## Dating Delinquents: Druggies and Dealers

My life became an effort in alliteration; you know, pushing things that start the same way together; in this case, in an endless stream of sex and drugs. All to avoid the pain that came when I thought about Jen—the true sting of love in our almost-never and our always-seldom, this was when I turned to taking hardcore drugs—to block it out. To not remember the things that had happened for years on end between us. The things that friends just don't do. But I'm not blaming her, only my stupid heart... Lots and lots of drugs... The easiest way to get them is either dating a drug addict or a dealer. When given the choice, I tried both. There was Wink, the guy who could make me orgasm for days on end while rolling, and "Kanaka" Dave, the best coke dealer, especially when he would shut the doors and the phones off and get high with me until the next payday hit. Then there was Sean, my rolling buddy with benefits, who was a low time dealer; he enjoyed rolling with me in the bedroom all night while the party screamed on. When it came to learning to forget, I had become a pro. No matter what I wanted, there was a man there in my life to fuck me stupid and get me high. But throughout all of this, I wanted more. I always do. All I really wanted was her.

#TheHeartWantsWhatItWants

# Chapter 10

# The Rave Movement Begins

Ⓟ Ⓛ Ⓤ Ⓡ

I think it's important to go backwards to go forwards, so I will take this time to tell you about the raver movement that became so predominant in the 1990s, and the underground lifestyle that became a part of my adolescent identity. An identity that—even after the flash of the glowsticks and the whirl of the telescreens faded away—still plays a special part in the person that I am today.

I learned about the Florida Rave Scene in 1995. The movement even came with its own mantra: Peace, Love, Unity, and Respect (P.L.U.R).

With my eighteenth birthday fast approaching, I began to go to more underground clubs than I can even count. Almost nightly, I would find myself geared up in soft cotton raver t-shirts and strong baggy denim JNCOs jeans, staying up until all hours of the early morning, and dancing to "Breakbeats", which I would learn later in life were a Florida treasure that most of the country still knows nothing about. Note: If you find yourself curious, look up DJ Icey's version of Kaycee's "Escape", Willie Mix and Darrell

Nutt's "Without You (Dave London Mix), or Nalin and Kane's "Beachball" (DJ Icey Mix) and you will see exactly what I am talking about.

The one thing that you need to know about raves is that they were tailored to fit the musical styles that only existed in certain sections of the country. House music originated in the Chicago and New York areas, Trance came over from Europe and mainly went into Los Angeles, and other styles such as Jungle and Bass originated in Detroit. Breakbeat was the sound of Florida, most specifically found in Brevard, Orange, and Dade County. It was absolutely serendipitous, the way in which individual styles of techno influences only existed in certain communities, and yet shaped an entire generation's musical subculture; virtually impenetrable, it seemed, by other cities' styles. Florida was part of that beautiful musical bubble and every person who was there during the breakbeat era is only now beginning to see how truly special it was, when they travel around the country and its raves, never to find the same style of music again, or the vibe that came with it.

I had many spiritual experiences during the rave movement, too. I shared some of the deepest connections that humankind is capable of, sometimes with over a hundred and thirty thousand of my 'closest' friends—people I had never met before, and may never see again, and yet I was bonded to them instantly, in that brief moment in time, through music. One love, one beat, one heart.

It was a magical experience; I enhanced my own character traits through sharing soul parts of myself with Jen; I sat with three of my friends, Corbin, Porscha, and Dylan, under a visibly growing tree that went from being a bush to an all-enveloping tree cocoon of leaves in a matter of hours; I kissed a ridiculous amount of women, including both strangers and friends alike, and I learned a lot about myself in the process. I also became pretty good at what was known in the scene as "glowsticking": a dancing style in which a person wields 6" phosphorescent neon bars in order to design patterns in the air that are aesthetically pleasing, especially when viewing them under the influence of MDMA. It was a scene of dreamers, affection, and a loving celebration of life that we were all sharing with one another. A vision of what the world could be if we could only stop for a single moment and just pay attention to the music.

## Being a Lesbian Raver
## At the End of the Millenium

So far, I come off like a lost saint right? But that, too, is an illusion. The transmutations of my life that led me into and out of these angelic trances were far from the quintessential goodness that they seem to purport. I was your typical kid: a rebellious, partying thing, with the added pressures of being a grown up in my home and a needy child in my head. I went through the same trials and tribulations of college and love interests and changes, but with the added necessity of being a caregiver to my grandmother as she battled with, and eventually lost the battle over, COPD. Even though I spent many a night in total oblivion, at home, I still fulfilled every single responsibility. I deserved whatever release I could find. My idea of respite was being so messed up that I couldn't move from the floor of the rave club for most of the night. I was in a delusion of grandeur because I still got to spend even more time with Jen, and all the while being as far from my own reality as possible. The lights, the beating drums, the repetitive patterns of light and music, and the love. I can't forget the love. Albeit drug-induced for the majority of its duration, the truth is it was always very real for me. I felt a strong pull to be one with the world, with each of the other ravers, and to enjoy dancing to one beat. A t-shirt I owned at one time said it best:

"Video games don't affect kids. If Pacman had affected us as kids, we would all be running around in darkened rooms, munching on magic pills, and listening to repetitive electronic music." – Nintendo CEO. That about sums it up.

## Without a Cause and Without a Clue

We were the second generation of hippies. We knew what we stood for: we wanted to create a world that lived the P.L.U.R. movement, but we were incapable of change because we didn't stand for anything; just against everything in the mainstream. But in those special moments on the dance floor, with everyone dancing to the same beat, we were truly one. I have been to hundreds of clubs and raves throughout the entire United States in my lifetime; really too many to count. It would be impossible to capture the true essence of all of them, but as I write this, I will try to paint the picture for you so you can truly understand what it means to be at peace in the height of the rave movement:

## Rule Number One: There's Nothing Like Your First Time

It's like seeing into heaven and feeling one with the world. It's like floating in an orgasm, ever present, for almost eight hours straight. Its sweat and kisses and hands and beats pulsating through your body in rhythm; like satin bed sheets rubbing against your newly shaven skin; fingertips grazing against your neck, shivering tingles emanating from your spine. It's like every word is truth and every fear is dead, and all you can do is feel. This is what it feels like to be rolling on pure MDMA. This was my first true experience on uncut Ecstasy. Rabbit in the Moon, Crystal Method, and DJ Icey blared through subwoofers set up at different sections of the outdoor rave. As you walk through an endless sea of bodies; everyone is touching and loving and just happy and carefree. And you are standing in the middle of it all, at the center of the universe, just breathing; just taking it all in.

## Rule Number Two: Water is Life

If there is only one thing that you MUST remember, it is to drink water. Your body becomes overheated from such close proximity with so many people. It can be stifling. It also comes from the urge to dance for hours and hours, continuously, consistently, and without end. You wouldn't go into a gym and workout without hydration, so why would you do this on the dance floor? Water is your best friend on these nights, when you are giving a stranger a back massage; a glowstick in your hand, a blow pop in your mouth, and the smell of menthol and eucalyptus invigorating your own senses—the aroma coming from the euphoric blend of Newport cigarettes and Vicks inhalers that enhance the effects of the pill.

Fast forward four hours—that's when the fun really begins. All of a sudden, your body goes numb and a rush hits your every nerve. Your eyeballs roll to the back of your head and you just have to sit down because you can't take it anymore. There's an intense heat that warms your body from the inside out. Your teeth begin to jitter and your head moves up and down with every shiver, in rhythm to the beat; it's uncontrollable. Your eyes flicker back and forth in what's known to rave veterans as "hammer vision," a side effect of the drug in which your sight is warped into rapid vibrations and all you can see is what is in front of you: a circular tunnel, slightly skewed like those large mirrors they place in the corner walls of convenience stores. This is accompanied by heavenly body sensations, starting from your back and pulsing like a drum throughout your entire body. The sensation is like free falling while you sit against a wall—too high to move, and yet flying through the cosmos, simultaneously.

And then, like a firecracker, you explode. You just wanna dance! It is the most intense orgasm of the night. Lasting about twenty to thirty minutes, it reminds you what it feels like to be alive. If you are lucky, someone will come up, maybe a friend, maybe a stranger, and begin to touch you all over. When you fall like a feather back down to the floor, there's someone holding you from behind, loving on you, and someone standing in front of you, giving you a light show. Then someone takes you onto their back; laying across them you spin in endless circles, up and down, your arms stretched out, like Superman. You *are* flying. Your cigarette burns down to the filter, but you don't notice. All you see is the whirl of lights in front of you, faster than your brain can process. Nonstop music, flashing lights, glow sticks everywhere, hundreds of songs, and yet it seems to be the same song, your favorite song, and it never ends. You are right in the moment now, and everything around you becomes a part of you.

Everyone is in their own space for that moment in time, and yet you are part of their experiences too. You feed off of each other and the energy in the room. Then, you continue to dance while sitting still. Your body sways and swoons. It stays this way for a while until that song that turned you on at the beginning of the night plays again and beckons you back to the dance floor. You dance harder, faster, taking in every breath until the sun comes up and the night winds down. It's like that.

Flying, floating, fleeing, freezing, freeing, feeling...

I would spend the next eight years of my life walking in and out of shayed out rooms, reminiscent of opium dens, watching people love and dance and just be free. I gained a wealth of life experience and found a meaning for it all through raves. Later in life, when I would be with several new women in long term relationships, the one thing that stayed true was my passion for clubbing and the ridiculous amount of sexual energy that I was able to release, both in those relationships and right here in this moment, on the dance floor.

## Rule Number Three: We Are All Searching For Something

I also came to find that amazing things could happen at a rave and transform people into something even more beautiful. I met many special people on this journey, some of which may have only come into my life but for a moment, and yet they impacted my life, and my perspective, forever.

## Last Night a DJ Saved My Life

He was just some bare-chested boy with a backpack and a pair of green glow sticks. We met in Florida at a rave called "Cyberfest" during the summer of 2001. The music was pumping loudly and I was feeling it course through my veins. I leaned down to offer this fellow dancer some water. "What's your name?" I asked, my palms sweaty from a night of pure adrenaline. He smiled back at me and replied, "I'm Justin." We decided to step outside and sit down on the grass. The dew drops from their blades rustled against our skin as we found a nice spot to chat.

"Where are you from, Justin?" I asked. He handed the water bottle back to me.

"I'm from Sweden," he replied shyly. A million thoughts raced through my mind like the motor cross bikes that were whirling in the cage behind us.

"Wow! That's a long way to come for a rave!" I shouted, the music becoming louder as more dancers joined us in the garden. I was amazed that someone would travel thousands of miles simply to come to a dance party. I was soon to find out that it was so much more than that.

As the night progressed, Justin told me his story:

"Raving actually saved my life" he began. "If it wasn't for this, I would already be dead."

His words echoed through my mind as I turned to hug him. As he came into my embrace, a soft tear fell upon my shoulder. As we stood there in the dark, just dancing to *Last Night A DJ Saved My Life*, mixed by Richard Humpty Vission, Justin leaned over and whispered into my ear, "I was very depressed and had been suicidal, but attending raves and meeting new people makes me feel that life is worth living."

You never know when someone is going to come into your life and change the way that you look at things. Justin proved to me once again that music has healing power. He showed me that a group of individuals, coming together in love and in celebration of life can help heal the world. I learned a very valuable lesson that night. No matter who you are or where you come from, you can always make a difference and be a part of change. Justin's life was changed forever by going to raves and ultimately deciding not to commit suicide. My life was changed forever by going to raves, knowing him, and being one stepping-stone of his life's journey.

# Chapter 11

# In the Eye of the Hurricane

## Red Cross My Heart

Although I was turning into quite the party-goer, I never forsook my obligations. I balanced work, school, caregiving, and partying like a boss. There is a sense of calm, however, that comes over a person when they sit in the eye of a metaphorical hurricane. The eye walls can be deceiving. A sense of foreboding doom comes over you, but yet the light of penetrating hope wraps itself around you and discards the fear, leaving you unprepared for the rise and the fall. This reminds me of a story about my grandma that I hold dear to my heart. It was the night that I became a volunteer for the American Red Cross.

I've told this story a million times, but each time I do, I realize more and more how it wasn't my actual choice to do what I did. I was merely a vessel, an anchor for God, who was able, through his grace, to save some lives—even through my own life's restlessness.

It was 2004, during Hurricane Jeane. We were still living in our small apartment, which was located directly in the path of the hurricane. My grandmother was on oxygen at this point, so if the power went off, she would lose the very air that she needed to live. As a result, I had to relocate her to weather the storm. We packed up all our necessities and headed to an elementary school down the street which opened its doors as a Special Needs Shelter.

I remember sitting outside smoking a cigarette with a woman who had an oxygen tank, just moments before they would close the shelter doors for the duration of the hurricane. As I settled in with my grandma for a while, I read books, played video games, and did whatever else I could do to pass the time.

It started out as a 1 a.m. walk through the school, prompted by sheer boredom. My grandmother was fast asleep in the middle of the night, and I was caged in by the confines of lockdown. While walking aimlessly, I noticed a clamor towards one of the rooms. As I stepped into the doorway, I saw a vortex of wind cycling at the top of the room; papers scattering in cyclical patterns, computers shaking off tables like fine china crashing on the floor. I was witnessing an F1 tornado, barreling into the newly removed roof of the room at full speed. The shingles and boards had peeled off just like the lid of a sardine can. I knew at that moment that I was meant to be there. I immediately went to the Red Cross group leader and asked to become an honorary volunteer in this chapter of the Red Cross.

Things progressed quickly from bad to worse. More rooms were demolished by the violent hands of nature. By two in the morning, our group had diligently relocated the entire shelter of people into the elementary school's cafeteria. But the problems did not end there. We were not just concerned with the patients, but with the very supplies that were sustaining their lives.

Patients came to a Special Needs Shelter because they had to have power, medications, equipment, and supervision to survive. To ensure their survival, I went along with an emergency medical team into the very rooms that were exposed to the elements. We crawled through waterlogged rooms, retrieving any medical supplies that we could find (and labeling them as best we could) so that they would hopefully make their way back to their rightful owners. I ran down the hallways, trudged through knee-deep water, and dug through rubble and debris to help save a life or two. Then I went back to check on my grandmother in the cafeteria, and that was where we remained for over two hours until police cars, fire trucks, and ambulances finally arrived. These were the only viable options for driving through a hurricane. One by one, the emergency responders relocated all these people, including my grandmother, to another shelter—the school next door.

I'd like to share with you what it is like to walk in 130 M.P.H. winds. Your feet do not physically make it off of the pavement unless you are falling from them. You cannot simply just walk to a new shelter or drive a car there, because the wind and flying debris would eventually find creative ways to kill you, much like the elaborate trappings of the "Final Destination" movie franchise. The reinforcements of emergency vehicles for transport, then, became the only way to relocate. I helped the team for four days, through two relocations; the first to weather the storm, the next, to help in the aftermath, before power was restored to the city. But at the end of it all, I realized one important thing: I was truly blessed to be a part of this healing history.

#TheHeartWantsWhatItWants

# Chapter 12

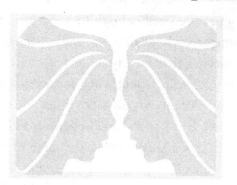

# The Many Loves of My So-Called Life

## Taking Control of My Sexual Prowess

Through all of the massive responsibilities, I also found time to nurture a quite robust sex life. Having been with countless men, I couldn't claim myself a gold star lesbian; you know, one who has only slept with other women—but I can say with full conviction that, among the myriad of men whom I shared a night's worth of bedding with, the main moments of my love life occurred with several beautiful ladies, and the unrelenting love for one woman, the one that I knew I would be in love with for the rest of my life. During the times in between, I found that being with a man made it hurt less, made it just sex, made it bearable on the nights when Jen was out with other friends and I wished that she was tangled up on my phone cord... and in between my thighs.

## Trolling on a Stranger's Tongue

I found my own ways to keep busy, to numb the pain. And yet again, I befriended people who were Jen's friends, even the somewhat perverted older man named Brad that Jen had known and flirted with during grade school. I guess in a way he was my confidant back in the day. No one could hold the emotion for this girl that I did, be as in love as I still was, even years later after the shine faded, and not have someone to speak to about it.

Someone who knew her well enough to know that I didn't make this whole story up. Someone who claimed to have feelings for her too. And through the in-between girlfriends, he would become a passing-the-time lover whom I became incredibly close with, and who, on several occasions, used me like I used him to help us both get over her. He was truly only interested in conquering her, but I...I was still hopelessly in love with her. Brad let me let that part of myself show, and at the same time released the dam that I had built up against its raging waters, the ones flowing through and outside of me, with his touch, with his tongue. While DJ Infiniti's break-beats pulsed in the background, one vocal track, "I Just Wanna Use Your Love Tonight", summed up our relationship perfectly. So whether it was the time when Brad and I had sex to that song while rolling at Parliament House, a gay club and motel rolled up into one, or just a lazy day of listening to music at his car dealership office where he ended up pleasuring me both with and without reciprocation, during one of the nights that I fucked him on the cold linoleum of an office floor, Brad reminded me that sex could just be simple, fun, and a pretty good way to temporarily forget everything. To forget her.

But on this one particular night, it all just started out with a bit of boredom and a not-so-thought-out plan. Drop some pills now, quickly head to Orlando, and see what the night had in store for us. It was on this night that I found myself again with Brad, so high that we couldn't make it ten minutes down the highway without pulling over in our borrowed limousine for what felt like an actual eternity.

As the pills kicked in, we were violently forced to let the overpowering waves of ecstasy rush through us on their due course. Brad finally regained control of his driving abilities a few hours later, as I continued to revel in my own ecstasy via MDMA-induced orgasms. As we finally got to Orlando hours later, we headed towards the downtown clubs. Standing in line outside a club, there was a couple in front of me, a boy and girl; the girl and I started talking, and out of nowhere, she leaned in and slid her tongue into my mouth. When it emerged, she had left a French kiss between my lips and a tab of acid on my tongue. At this point it might help to remember, I was already rolling. All I can remember of this night was dancing on the floor with Brad, spinning in circles, and then meeting Eric, my new soon-to-be rolling buddy, and Brad's friend Riley with his own friend, before getting back into our limousine to head back home. When I got there, Riley, Brad, and Eric went upstairs, while I laid downstairs on the floor, rolling balls with Riley's friend. All of a sudden, this sweet stranger asked me out of nowhere, "Can I eat you out?" Like a simple request. Something innocent that would feel good. I told him earlier that night that I was a lesbian, but he didn't care. His reply? "I just want to make you feel good. I like you." After humoring him for three hours and enduring several additional pleas from him to make love to me, I pushed his head away with a gentle "no" and held him in my arms, as we fell asleep with each other on a hard floor made of clouds.

See, the path to finding your way out of darkness is a long and winding road. Among the things that I shared with Jen, a severe depression state was the least desirable and yet the most prominent. Hers, I would come to find out, was a clinical condition. Mine, however, came from the simple act of loving her. I needed to move forward, even if I couldn't fully move on. This is when I found myself in the company of numerous women who pushed this pain far inside and eventually, if only for a moment in time, made it go away altogether.

# Interlude 1: The Women

## Sheila

Where to start? How about with Sheila, the sexy gothic goddess that I met during Rocky Horror. Let me explain: it was during a time when I would frequent a movie theater that did live shows, acting alongside the cult classic "The Rocky Horror Picture Show." Jen and I had become regulars there because her friend Kat was part of their makeup team. I lived at Rocky, watching Eddy, being acted out by my friend Ed, as he rode around on a fictitious motorcycle during an iconic scene in the movie. Sheila, Ed's girlfriend in real-life, was adorable. Once again, a woman with black hair, this time wavy, had captured my attention. Her green emerald eyes, slated like jade, would stand out to me even more a few months later, when she would stare provocatively at me during a neighborhood party.

I was standing in the bathroom, putting lipstick on, when she walked in. I had been flirting with her across the room for hours, and as she walked up to me and, without saying a word, simply kissed me, the world fell away from us. We started to make out passionately, banging against walls and doorways, falling headfirst over a couch and onto the carpet...we rolled ourselves back up and out the door to continue all the way to the next apartment which, luckily for us, was hers. We continued clumsily banging into things to the amusement of her roommate Tina, another woman whom I had experienced a slight sexual liaison with. Sheila and I ended up on her twin bed, making love until sunlight, when I would find myself getting dressed to her naked shadow and walking out the door.

You see, after our night of passion, Sheila had made it quite clear that she did not believe in relationships. She was not a monogamous person and was not willing to try a committed bisexual relationship. I was not willing to settle for anything less. I told her that this could never happen again, kissed her goodbye, and walked home.

Little did I know that twenty minutes later I would be staring into her eyes again.

As I settled in to do some online surfing of the internet, I heard a knock on my door. I turned around from my computer desk, expecting my grandmother to come walking in...but it was Sheila, who entered my room and walked up to me, this time kissing me again and saying "OK. I'll give it a try." Maybe the sex was just that good, or maybe she was really feeling me the same way that I was feeling her. It was probably just the sex. Right?

At this time in my life, I was also unemployed, just trying to make my way through college. I didn't let this stop me, however, from making money to treat my girlfriend to the finer things in life. I would even go so far as to enroll in 'Daily Work, Daily Pay', an organization set up for the unemployed so that they could at least earn a day's paycheck by doing manual labor. I lifted bricks and worked on construction sites during the morning hours just so I could spend my nights intoxicated, dancing at a club, or just relaxing at home with her; really doing whatever we wanted to.

## The Night Brad and I Threw a Rave

If I'm going to tell the story of Sheila in all of its glory, I must also talk about how our interaction, like those that me and countless other girlfriends shared, crashed into a meeting with Jen. She was the one destiny that kept coming back to me. And we always seemed to come together just when it felt like everything else was falling apart.

It was a week like any other; me hanging out with Brad and trying to find trouble. This time, however, we yearned to make it for ourselves. We decided to throw a rave. As we hung black lights and set up turntables, I could sense a night to remember coming into view. We printed out massive copies of fliers for our underground party and started letting people know about it. As the night came upon us, I found myself in the office of Brad's car dealership, VIP status, with Sheila in tow.

And who else would be joining us of course than Jen, walking into our rave right at the very moment when Sheila was watching porn on Brad's big screen and making out with me, rough style on the couch. I was too far gone to even move, as Jen spent a few minutes in the room, barely acknowledging my presence, and then found herself running around with the many so-called loves of her own life.

Our party came to an abrupt end when the cops showed up an hour or so later. But as they attempted to shut down the rave, Brad informed them that he was merely holding a private car sale, and there was music for incentive. His office, after all, was in a business district, and as such, they couldn't touch us. We remained in the office, completely 'innocent' of any 'provable' wrong-doing. About ten minutes in, as everyone left through the gates to the garage, Sheila and I decided to jump ship as well, and we found ourselves back at her home, tangled in bed with one another, trying out the new moves we had learned from the porn stars which defined our lust for one another that night.

I was really good at pushing Jen to the back of my mind; proving that I could go out without her, and it wouldn't hurt. That I could sleep with someone else, and not her, and that I could live my own life, separate from hers; that I wouldn't think about her. But drugs and sex do that too.

## Getting Back to the Girl

One of those drugged up nights stands out in my mind more than any other. The night that Sheila and I went out to Club Harmony, rolled all night, and then drove out to the beach. We were the vision of perfection, as we sat on the boardwalk stairs, simply cradling one another in each other's arms to a backsplash spectrum of picturesque sunrise.

But all good things, when they are not destined, must come to an end. Sheila ended things with me on a crazy note. She broke up with me suddenly, citing her non-desire to be with a woman anymore as her reasoning. She moved away to Virginia, but not until we truly had our last moment together. It was during a party downstairs from my apartment that I was invited to. The boys that lived there had seen how heartbroken I was and suggested that I come to their kegger to help me forget and move on. Little did I know that they also invited Sheila to celebrate her last night in town before her departure the next morning.

Here we saw each other after almost a full week of no contact, and I tried desperately to keep my distance. At about three a.m. that morning, she approached me and said she wanted to talk. We went upstairs to the third-floor roof and kissed intensely for almost an hour. At the end of our make out session, Sheila told me the true reason that she was leaving. "I think I'm falling in love with you" she said, "and I don't wanna be with a woman for the rest of my life." As I walked away and Sheila walked out of my life forever, I was left with the Verve's "Bittersweet Symphony" playing round and round in the record player of my mind. Looking at her Facebook page now, I can see that she got everything out of the "hetero- American Dream" that she wanted...a man to marry, a white-picket fence, and 2.5 kids (well three, technically speaking.) I'm happy for her. It is only a shame that she had to deny that part of her heart to get it.

## Jessica

Along with the good side of raving, comes the bad. I experienced this with a woman whom I had known for years. While working with Jen at Action Research, I became friends with several misfits. Among them was Corbin, a cute guy who reminded me of a chubby Kurt Cobain, and whom I did, on a few occasions, share my bed with. Between ice, fire, and candle play, Corbin awoke me to another side of my sexual self: one that could simply be pleasured by a man without any intentions of reciprocation. As a result, I did give in on several nights and rewarded my man slave for a job well done.

During our time at work, Corbin was dating a girl named Jessica. She was truly beautiful—adorable with blond wavy hair, and lusciously long legs. One day, he told me that she thought I was cute and wanted to hang out. They proceeded to invite me to a live action role play game, during which I kissed her for the first time.

That night, we were sitting at a table, surrounded by maps, dice, and gaming books. I sat across from her, looking up every so often to see a soft smile upon her face gazing straight back up at me. I felt her foot slightly brushing, grazing up against mine, and I could tell that this was the beginning of something.

Corbin called me into a bedroom and asked me if I wanted to talk to her. "Of course," I replied. He went to get her and when she walked into the room, she quietly came up to me and gently kissed my lips.

We spent the next few months at her house every weekend, getting to know each other slowly and in detail. She had never been with a woman romantically, so as we explored each other, her timidity and my own chivalry kept me just above the belt-buckling bridge of no return. I laid in her bedroom for hours, making out with her, staring at the art she created on the wall. She was a painter, creative and eclectic, and she made me feel like I was beautiful, like I was part of her art. She took me away from the pain of Jen's rejection and helped me see that it, all of it, was her loss. Weeks turned into months, and months moved into years.

One night, I invited Jessica to Cyberzone with me, a club that I would frequent about three times a week, attempting to forget everything, and feel everything, at the same time. This night, however, must have been tainted by evil, as what I would encounter on our weekend trip was broken dreams and shattered reality. And I would find myself once again, by the end of the night, lucky to be alive.

We started our weekend excursion renting a hotel room and picking up a dime bag for Jessica. I would then proceed to find other recreational items that would give me the worst experience of my life thus far. We were in the club, feeling it, feeling each other, and feeling the effects of the MDMA that was running through our bloodstream. At around four a.m., I brought her out to my car, and told her, for the first time, "I love you." I then began to explain that I did not feel comfortable there anymore and I asked her to leave and go back to the hotel with me. She responded, "If you love me, you'll let me stay." This was the first time she had taken a break from her own convictions when it came to being against the chemical alterations of drugs, so I accepted her request. In the back of my mind, however, I knew something wasn't right. I would soon find out what true terror was.

As we finally were leaving the club at five a.m., two boys walked up to us and asked if we wanted to go party at their house. Even though I quickly rejected the offer, Jessica begged me to go. Maybe she needed to exert her "straightness." For whatever reason, we checked out of our hotel, the dumbest move ever, and drove over to their house. I made sure to take my car, which was the one thing that truly saved us.

We got to the house and started hanging out with the boys in the bedroom. Jessica was in her element. We started making out hardcore, ripping each other's clothes off. I was so into her. Then I noticed that her attention had turned to one of the boys. I tried to get her to go downstairs, but she wouldn't budge. The second guy asked me to come downstairs with him. I followed.

He brought out a silver tray with enough dope to kill a horse. "I know you are a true veteran of the scene. You can have as much as you want. Just know that if you stop what's going on right now, I will kill you." I freaked out. It turns out I don't do very well with death threats. I even sat on this boy's lap, watching the sun come up, and then watching Jessica walk down the stairs like a true angel, dressed in nothing but the other boy's boxers.

It hurt my heart so much that I couldn't protect her. I would have raged if I could have, but my body was partially paralyzed and my mind was in shock. I stayed put.

I went to the bathroom to take a hot shower, trying to wash the bad scene out of me. When I reached for the shampoo, I didn't find any liquid. I found flies. I freaked out, tripping hard. I dried off and joined everyone in the front room. Next, I went through a CD book which had a lot of cool CDs, and at the back part, the part he only showed me, a memorial notice of a thug friend of theirs who died. I got the feeling that I was part of some wicked gang initiation. This just made me wig out even more. The boy who had been with Jessica decided to go to the store and asked if we wanted anything. By this time the sun had come out, and I wanted a bottle of wine to forget the pain I was going through.

When he came back, he had changed clothes. He asked us if we wanted to go into the Jacuzzi, but I was afraid to shock my system with hot water again. Finally, I convinced Jessica to leave, but we had nowhere to go, and I was in no true condition to drive. We ended up at a smaller motel with the last of the money I had, and I proceeded to notice her breathing weird and freaked out. I called an ambulance to come make sure she was ok. Instead, I received one of Florida's finest knocking on the bedroom door.

When they asked to see her, all that they did was ransack the room. The dime bag we had not even opened was sitting there out in the open for them to discover in her purse. I tried to take responsibility for it, but the cop just said "I'm taking one of you to jail. If you wanna go with her, keep talking, but she's going anyway, whether you talk or not." I felt completely devastated. I had needed help and they had just sent the cops. I had tried to save her the entire night, and all it did was cause more problems. She had a good job with a government contract. I knew she would lose everything: her parents' respect, her job, and her good name. I left her that morning, after the cop decided to issue her a citation for court, and she chose to call her parents and walk out of my life, but not forever. A few years later, we ran into each other online, and she became a long-distance friend. Luckily, she had gotten into college despite our terrifying indiscretions, and I couldn't be happier for her, even though straightening out her life meant she had to leave mine.

## Vicki

*I can't tell you that it is easy to write this part. It's not. Vicki, unfortunately, is no longer with us. God gave her angel wings in early 2000. But the memories that I hold of her will live on forever in my heart.*

I met Vicki while I was dating my boyfriend, Steve. Even though he played a significant role in my life, our relationship came out of a trashy romance novel. We began dating over booze, karaoke, and women, and that is exactly how life remained for almost three years. During our last conversation when I finally ended it, Steve revealed to me that I was the only woman he ever considered marriage with, which made the end of our relationship that much more bitter than sweet. Steve was an amazing partner in that he knew deep down inside that I was a lesbian and wanted to give me what I wanted. Now I can't say that he didn't benefit from this, but, in all reality, a straight woman could have never stayed with a playboy like Steve.

Our arrangement was simple: He would meet them in a bar, we would all dance together. He would ask her over to dinner one night, and as I played soft piano music in the background, the mood would set itself. After dinner, a beautiful Jacuzzi tub awaited, along with another bottle, typically rum or whiskey, and this scenario would always end the same way: with Steve and I waking up to a beautiful woman on the right side of a bed built for three.

Vicki, then, started as a simple conquest. The same tired lines, the same cheap wines. The difference, however, is that I really liked her. A lot. She was absolutely drop dead gorgeous and had a heart of gold. She was a true philanthropist, donating her wealth to many organizations and partaking in several fundraisers for local charities. Truth is, in retrospect, she was conquering me. Beating me at my own game then, she made the first move. During a night of drinking and dancing, she joined Steve and I on the dance floor, and propositioned to come home with us. She needed a man, but she wanted me.

I remember feeling like a child laying in the hot tub with her. I was the nervous one. Every time I would back away a little, she would scoop me up and hold me, kissing my neck and lips until I couldn't move. Then, wrapped in her arms, I would gently lower my lips to her breast, and run my hands down between her thighs, afraid no more. I can still feel her thumb against my lips before plunging her tongue in my mouth. I can see myself, looking back up into her baby blues with an innocent hunger. I can feel the heat of the Jacuzzi and the buzz of the whiskey or wine, and her hands, endlessly searching my body while I searched back with my own.

There was a cardinal house-rule to threesomes: our lovers, they could share us, they could share our bed, but as the Queen of my own castle, I would always sleep in the middle. Vicki was the exception. I would come to let her own the bed in the same way that she owned me.

Our love affair was brief and yet, in those quiet moments when Steve would be off playing tennis, and I would be sharing the house with my own Queen, it was infinite; natural. We would drift into the ocean of our bed, while she sang The Beach Boys: "Surfer Girl" softly into my ear, and I didn't have to speak much with her in return—all I had to do was feel. I was ever present in every moment, including the one that came only a few months later and a lifetime too soon.

Vicki was diagnosed with lung cancer only two months before she passed away. At the ridiculously young age of thirty-two, she was dying from something terminal; something I couldn't fix, and all I could do was pray. This wonderful woman who donated all of her time and money to help make the world a better place, this amazing treasure who shared my heart, and my bed, was dying.

I prayed for her. I did a Wiccan ritual to bless a candle of lavender and jasmine with healing energies to stop her pain. The last time I talked to her was via a phone in her hospital room, when she thanked me for the candle, said she had not been in any pain thanks to the candle (as I was too innocent at the time to realize that her pain was also being muted by morphine). She told me that she loved me very much. And then she was gone. She was a brilliant star before I even knew her; a supernova, fading away way too fast for me to catch her. To catch a falling star.

## Hope

Hope had an interesting role in my life. She was a friend, a lover, a spiritual adviser, and a healer. During the rough times with Jen, which were ongoing throughout several of my relationships, I found myself in a very strange place spiritually. I felt an evil impetus from Jen; partially from the way that she treated me, and partially by her own admission to dabbling with the dark side of the occult. During her teenage years, she had participated in some nasty anti-religious things with several friends and even a few exes, and the true impact of that choice was now affecting me, the person who still loved her. I felt a dark soul sickness which was slowly draining me of the person I had become, strangling my very breath from my chest.

*I must note here, I don't know if this is even something that most people will believe possible. It happened though, so anyone else's feelings about it are irrelevant to that fact. Like Kelly Clarkson says, "Will you love me, even with my dark side?"*

*Many years later, I would forgive Jen for what had been her evil doings, but to this day, I do not know if she truly knows the spiritual battle that we fought with each other parallel to this world in what can only be described as the Netherrealm of the cosmos; breaking through the fourth wall of our own existence.*

Hope and I had been online friends for a while. I wasn't attracted to her by looks initially, but more so by the connection that we shared religiously. Hope had been part of the Wiccan faith, during a time when I was questioning the extent of my own. Even though I know I am a Christian, I also believe some of the core tenements of Wicca because I know the spiritual power that the world holds through my own witnessing of both life's white and black magics.

While Hope and I were officially together as a couple, I still harbored feelings for Jen, but she and I were, just like the Journey song, starting to go our "Separate Ways". Hope knew everything about me, about my love for Jen—seemingly unrequited—and she still accepted me for who I was, even with my undying flame.

This was how it all happened: I found myself very ill one day, feeling as if my chest would explode. Hope suggested that I come out to California to do a ritual with her small coven, and I accepted. I won't go into too much detail (some things must remain sacred), but the four of us stood at the beach as I watched a glowing green gunk get removed from my body via a violent surgery with a piece of driftwood while I was standing wide awake and within the protection of the circle.

Afterwards, Hope nursed me back to health, slowly, and I became better than I was before. Hope, on the other hand, became much worse. She had been battling with diabetes for years, and not taking care of herself very well led her to having blood sugar ranges in the 300 level that became life threatening. After endless trips to doctors and day long waits at the L.A. County Hospital, Hope was not getting any better. Our love life also became mostly one sided and our friendship became strained because Hope simply could not fulfill my insatiable sexual needs. We had even gone so far as exchanging rings, but this attempt at an engagement was not right, and resulted in my swift return to Florida, a month before I had intended. Even though we ended the relationship, we would stay friends for many years to come.

## Sandy

She came into my life like a lion and left like a lamb. Just as many of the greatest relationships come about through friendship, so did ours. I met Sandy at a house party hosted by one of my coworkers. Meeting her was both mysterious and seemingly inconsequential. Not even in my periphery, I was just getting over Hope and just looking for kind company and good conversation. Instead, I would find myself courted by an actual dating ritual and romantically wooed over several months by a woman for the first time in my life who wanted to take it slow.

Sandy was strictly a platonic friend. I knew that she was straight and that gave me the emotional freedom to truly be myself with her. I told her all about my past life and lovers and she eagerly pressed me to open up to her even more. One evening while we were hanging out late at her friend's house where she was staying, I ended up sleeping over. Being unprepared for a slumber party, I asked to borrow her pajamas. After I finished getting dressed, Sandy walked into the room and stripped completely naked before crawling into bed with me. This is when she also chose to tell me that she was bisexual. Sensing that I might be uncomfortable, she asked if she should get dressed again. Of course, I responded "no", being that it was her home and her bed, who am I to question how she chooses to sleep? Sandy simply kissed me on the cheek, and we went to sleep, cuddled up in each other's arms. As friends. Period.

We went out for ice cream the next day and, for some strange reason, it felt like a date. Eventually, we began working at a telemarketing call center with each other too, something that seemed to be a pattern of mine. We also started to go out dancing after work on Thursdays at a club called Coral Bay. We would continue to find ourselves on many a night having drunken slumber parties—always sleeping in the same bed, the same way, night after night. After a while, I started to get comfortable sleeping nude too. I started to officially date her about six months after we met, and it would be another few months before we would end up in bed together, this time on the right side of wrong.

The weekend that we made love for the first time seemed to come out of an after-school special. She invited me over to her parent's house where she was watching their cats.

"My parents will be gone for the weekend" she whispered slyly in my ear during work one night, as she winked at me with her shimmering blue eyes. Gosh was I a sucker for blue eyes.

"Would you like to come over this weekend?"

That Friday afternoon, we pulled into the driveway with a heavy sense of anticipation for the weekend to come. When we had settled in a bit, we sat on the couch and watched *Aladdin* together, cuddled up in each other's arms. As it ended, we sang "A Whole New World" to each other, me with my

Jasmine by my side. Then we began to kiss. I brought my gaze up and saw that look in her eyes as we both glanced in unison at the stairway leading to her room upstairs.

I loved the way that her bedroom ceiling vaulted over the bed, like it was enveloping us in a protective love-making shroud. With Sandy's head between my thighs, I started to feel like Alice, falling down the rabbit hole. That is the only way to describe the sensation. Sandy, like a little pixie fairy, was fluttering around me, kissing and touching, and I slowly delved into this, non-seemingly but nonetheless, X rated world of innocence, beauty, sex, and fairy tales. We went at it for hours, spending the entire weekend christening every room of her parent's house, including their bed. It was a magical relationship that would endure for two and a half years, the longest declared relationship I had been in at that point of my life. But still not the longest time that I had been in love.

## Interlude 2: Choosing a Side - Fixing the Broken Pieces

During Sandy and I's relationship, I was hanging out with Jen off and on. One night, Jen and I went on a trip to the beach; one in which my spiritual self had called upon us. I asked her to choose a side, good or evil, to war for her soul. The feeling of possibly impending Armageddon, as it is known in the Bible, was palpable.

Her answer to me was that she was going to "straddle the fence." This was not an option. The choice to not choose good, regardless of its extent, to me, is an indirect decision towards evil. What's more, I could feel the influence of her spiritual negativities in my own life now and the damage her darkside did to my heart. We were bound by this indescribable love that had survived throughout endless relationships, and yet we were never together but never apart.

Sandy and I did a ritual of judgment, in which I poked pins dipped in black paint in a fresh lemon. The idea was that each pin was a wrong that Jen had inflicted on me (fourteen specific offenses over the years), and I was calling God

(Goddess) to give her instant karma, both good and bad, for those wrongs. I wanted to help her wipe the slate clean, to give her soul a chance to rebuild on a clean foundation but, in the religion of Wicca, doing so has a cost. You must also accept your own wrongs and pay for them too. And I did. Dearly.

Jen was robbed at work later that year. Jen got a brand-new Mustang out of the settlement from that case. Her married girlfriend cheated constantly on her. Her romance ended, but so did her evil tendencies. Years later, Jen would make the ultimate sacrifice for others by becoming a nurse. *She would then choose to right her wrongs through religion and her decision to do good makes me never regret mine to save her.*

Meanwhile, Sandy and I moved in together at my grandma's house (a huge step, by the way, for an elderly woman who just a few years ago thought that I was just going through a "phase"). She even bought us, *two women*, a new bed and headboard so we could spend our nights back in my childhood home, making love and falling asleep in each other's arms, while my grandmother lay outside, sleeping on the couch.

About a year later, we started singing karaoke three times a week. One night outside our favorite bar haunt, the new lesbian butch in town, Bobbie, started flirting with us and I started playing with fire. This flirtation would end in a three-way relationship in which I received the short straw. Sandy broke up with me on Christmas morning at a small diner on the beachside, holding hands with Bobbie, telling me she was not in love with me anymore, as I drove the two of them back to her house and drove back to mine, alone.

I spent the next night with Jen, in the middle of a wondrous possibility—a moment to realize my need for her, my desire. But as she kissed me with the tenderness of a butterfly, I still felt the sting of Sandy's betrayal. Even more so, I now knew that everything I had ever thought was true, which made it even worse. Jen did love me too. She may have even been in love with me at some point. I could feel it in her kiss. I ran, as fast as I could, into the arms of another woman. But not before spending the night with Jen, wrapped tightly in her arms. But I couldn't stay; I just couldn't bear to be hurt again the way she had hurt me before.

**Aylie**

A few days after Sandy, I ended up going online again, looking for someone to talk to who knew where I was coming from and understood what I had just been through. That was where I met Aylie.

It started as an innocent talk, which she wanted to take further. I was reluctant to give out my phone number to another stranger, but something reassured me that I was doing the right thing. She called me that night while playing the video game "Silent Hill" with her friends, all the while chatting like we were the only ones in the room. After an innocent discussion about Disneyland versus Walt Disney World, I knew that she was someone I wanted to get to know better, and someone who could make me *feel* again. I had just ran away, yet again, from the only woman I had truly ever wanted to be with, and I just needed some time to figure it all out, away from her, where I could breathe.

Aylie sent me a picture with her and three other girls and told me she was the one on the left. It turned out she was on the left half of the picture, but so was the girl I had mistaken her for. Aylie was from California, and as the days progressed, we began a long-distance relationship with each other. We quickly fell in what we thought was love but I would later find out was actually sex addiction, and I went out to California yet again, this time to meet the woman who would absorb the next five years of my life.

If Sandy and I's relationship was a fairytale, then Aylie and I's relationship could be described as a triple XXX adult film. We met for the first time at the airport, and I was shocked to discover that she was not the girl I expected her to be. Nonetheless, we couldn't keep our hands off of each other. Even though I found no real physical attraction to her, the sexual attraction built on our emotional premise was primal and magnetic. We immediately began a drive to visit with my old friend Shawn from Georgia. He was stationed in California after going into the Marines, and this trip was also an awesome way for us to catch up. As we drove the two hours towards San Diego, our hands groping, fingers sliding over the denim between our legs, Aylie and I fought back the urge to rip each other's clothes off and just pull off the road.

Somehow, we made it to our hotel room still clothed. We started kissing in the hallway of the hotel, over the threshold of the door, and fell onto the bed, still tied together by our tongues. We woke up from a true Delta sleep still kissing each other over two hours later. That was an amazing experience. When I asked her what she had seen in her dreams, while kissing me, she saw a palm tree with a beautiful beach landscape and a rainbow in the sky over us. This was the same thing that I had dreamt with my lips parted and my tongue still tangled with hers. We then had passionately endless sex until the next day, and every night for years to come.

## Interlude 3: Not Everyone is Gay in San Diego

Even though I was told how gay friendly and open-minded San Diego was, I saw firsthand how this logic only extended so far. It was a few days into my trip to Cali, and I was hanging out with Aylie, Shawn, and his then-boyfriend in the outdoor hotel Jacuzzi. Out of nowhere, Shawn decided to become bold and have his boyfriend give him head. Suddenly, we heard shouting coming from a window upstairs, and the next thing we knew, a man was screaming that he was "gonna beat our asses." As we sat there, frozen with panic, two men came barreling down to where we were. Even though what Shawn did was wrong in public, their reaction to it was downright dangerous.

I had heard about deadly gay bashings before and, looking into the eyes of the people screaming at us, I thought for sure we were about to experience one firsthand. Aylie and I were topless, so getting dressed was not that difficult, but the boys were naked and they took a few drawn out minutes to get dressed while the guys stood over us—steam seeming to come out of their ears, and a strange bulge in the shape of a gun protruding from the waistline of their sweatpants. We went back to our room quickly, not looking back on what could have been the quintessential end for all involved.

Aylie and I also became engaged during this trip. During a lovely autumn afternoon, we took a stroll into West Hollywood and were just window shopping inside the store, when a beautiful store employee came up to us with a Polaroid camera and two glasses of champagne. Somehow, he just knew. It was fated: he appeared with an impromptu setting for our picturesque engagement. We picked out these two inexpensive rings made of titanium and proposed to each other right in front of our cashier witness. I went back to Florida later that week, with full intentions on seeing this relationship through and still taking care of grandma in the process, until it would be time for her to go to heaven and for me to move to California permanently.

#TheHeartWantsWhatItWants

# Chapter 13

# Missed Opportunities

## Kissing Friends

Meanwhile, my friendship with Jen was also being repaired, for the second time. I had spent less time with her during my relationship with Sandy, and it took its toll on us. I went out with her and her girlfriend Rita to several clubs or raves while I was in a long-distance relationship with Aylie, and one evening at Club Firestone, it got real.

I should mention that when I am raving, I sometimes get caught up in the moment. I had kissed Jen's girlfriend Rita during many a rave, as it was just part of the experience. Even Jen had no problem with it, at least not to my knowledge. One night we were all out at a club together, and I was sad when I heard "Toxic" by Britney Spears being remixed by the DJ. I told Rita and Jen that the song reminded me of my ex, Sandy, because it was the song that Bobbie had seduced us to. Rita calmly grabbed my hand and told me that "she would fix that..." Looking back, Jen just sat there, smoking a cigarette on the large brick planter outside the club with a huge grin on her face, as Rita led me back through the side door. Inside, a piece of chain link fencing was placed against one of the walls, and Rita pinned me up to it and began to give me a show, weaving around my body like a stripper; once again, a woman pinning my hands while they took charge. As the song changed, Rita kissed me at the end of it, and to this day, that is exactly the memory I hold of that song.

Later in the early morning hours, after I had returned home and retired to bed, and after falling asleep mangled on the phone with Aylie, Jen and Rita went down to the beach to share intimate time with each other. I was later told by Aylie that they broke through the phone line via the emergency operator and had asked me to come down to the beach to enjoy their company and to bring some adult toys. I can't say for sure what I would have done if I had been awake enough to take the call, but I do know the pain that came to my heart when Aylie told me she hung up on them and I was left with the droning thought of *what if I had just stayed...* Yet another missed opportunity to intimately share my love with the woman that I loved—the one whom I have always loved.

## Interlude 4: Running On Empty While Trying To Change The World

No matter what's going on inside me, or what's happening around me, I am always the person who makes sure that the people in my life are safe and cared for—in mind, in body, and in spirit. I guess, then, that it is no surprise that the idea of being "Florence Nightingale," as my grandmother put it, started in my youth. Not only had I been the savior of many girlfriends and the resolver of their problems, I had also been called to teach—to shape the world with my God-given gifts.

It was a rough road, back and forth from being the caregiver of my aging grandmother, to working fourteen-plus-hour-day jobs and managing full-time college, all simultaneously, but I made it work. Moreover, I had made a vow to help my grandmother and keep her out of a nursing home. This had been her dream. Her final wish. I would go on to take care of the one who took care of me, keep our family afloat financially, and work towards that teaching credential, scraping through dirt and climbing through fire. After a while, my own version of the "American dream" started to crash.

By the age of ninety-two, my grandmother was on her deathbed and I, now merely twenty- four, sat frozen in the corner, losing my mind. "I can't keep this up," I would tell myself, but that was little consolation to the minimum nursing help I could get out of the state and the mounting list of medications and doctors' visits that became final life support to a dying organism.

## Interlude To The Death Of A Dream

A moment of silence for my grandmother: Mildred Thomas Sennyes (1914-2005)

*Thank you.*

# Chapter 14

# A Prophecy Fulfilled

## Rushing Home to Save Her

On vacation, while visiting Aylie, my grandmother suffered a heart attack and became quite ill. She was rushed from the rehabilitation facility that she had been in for about a month—after a major bout with her emphysema—to Wuesthoff Hospital. I returned back into town, with Aylie, the day of my College graduation, which I had set up early via the permission of my college board because I knew grandma was fading and that it had been her life's dream to see me graduate college.

*When I was seventeen, I had a genuine conversation with God; in that visionary moment, I was told that she would die very soon after my college graduation.*

Flash back to that day—the one in which I flew back from California, just a few hours shy of my college graduation. When we arrived, the hospital told me that my grandmother couldn't leave, but grandma and I had different plans and we decided that I would "break her out" anyways. We contacted her primary care physician who gave the green light to our prison break, knowing how much it would mean to her to see me graduate, and even though the doctor on call at the hospital would not discharge her, the nurses would still see us run down the hallway with her in a wheelchair—my grandmother smiling from ear to ear, hurtling our way towards freedom. And as I slipped her into my '79 Buick, I didn't look back.

When we got to the ceremony, I rushed to get in line with my peers and Aylie took my grandma with the wheelchair to the top of the stadium room where she would fit. Aylie later told me that, as they called my name to receive the diploma, my grandmother squeezed her hand hard and smiled, with a tear running down her face. Later, when she would be at home after our celebration dinner at Carrabas, my grandma would playfully toss the graduation balloons that I had received up into the air. For that one day, she wasn't sick at all.

She became a kid again.

## Happiness Doesn't Last Forever

I was there the night she told me she was done; the night she refused food, water, and medications, and I was there the day the hospice bed arrived, **two** days after it was originally scheduled to be delivered... and **one** day after grandma fell off the couch at six in the morning. Fucking hospice! There is no doubt in my mind that my grandmother broke several body parts that were never identified because her last wish, as previously stated, was to not die in a hospital, and I was not about to go back on my promise. With her DNR posted in plain view next to the wall phone, twenty plus firemen still forcefully tried to convince me otherwise. They spoke to me sternly and harshly, telling me that as the Power of Attorney I could still override her wishes, and implying that if I didn't, I was nothing more than a murderer. They stood locked into position around the cracked marble coffee table that broke my grandma's fall that morning, and I stood, crumbling, holding firm to her last wishes.

"Let her stay here at home" I responded to them—she being broken-winged and I, broken-hearted.

If I'm going to keep telling it, I might as well cleanse my soul of that last day, the one that repeated for years and years like a broken record through my mind, looping through time... I can see it even now; a dusty record with deep jagged grooves and a needle stuck in just one, always playing back the day.

My grandmother, too, pulled the cord on the phonograph of her own life, and, just like that night, she gave a death rattle to the sound of "Unforgettable" by Nat King Cole, as I played it on my piano. That and the hand-holding serenade I gave of an acapella version of "Silent Night" by Boyz II Men that came right after, the one in which death took her by the time I had sung the second verse, sending down the archangel Michael to hand her the reins to her brand new golden chariot and her very own pair of gilded wings.

## Surviving the Fires of Hell

I was in shambles. I could not stay in the place where I had been with her on her deathbed—the place that I could not call a home without her in it. My friend Sasha offered me her home, just as she had done before for my grandmother and I during another hurricane—the one which made me swear to never put her in a shelter again. I spent the next four months in a depressed blur, trying desperately not to do stupid things like drink the bottle of liquid morphine that I still had after grandma's passing. I spent Christmas Eve with Sasha at a big party in which we lit a candle and celebrated my grandmother's life with over thirty people who never knew her. I mourned silently, in Sasha's room, under crocheted blankets, avoiding almost everyone, including Jen, who I could not **bare** to let into this part of my life. I couldn't open up enough to let her back in, just when I needed her the most, because I couldn't handle being with Aylie, dealing with my grandmother's death, living with Sasha, and still being in love with Jen at the same time.

Sasha did her absolute best to distract me and to be the most selfless best friend I have ever had in my entire life. She spent all kinds of money and time on me to help me forget, showered me with gifts, and gave me nights of entertainment, calling over all of my friends one or two at a time to come over and hang out. She helped me to move past the suicidal tendencies and the deep depression that had taken me over completely.

# The Cleansing Fire

In April, just days before I was leaving to move to California, I had a dream that I was on fire. I could even smell my flesh burning, it was that real. I started to scream in my dream, and as I woke up I realized, it was not a dream at all. The bed, my cell phone, and my arm were literally on fire. I jumped up, screaming at the top of my lungs. I vaguely remember Sasha putting me out with a blanket, washing the burn a bit, and then rushing me off to the Wuesthoff Emergency Room. The same hospital that I had broken grandma out of just months before was now my current destination of choice. It turns out that my cell phone, the one that I had plugged into the wall and nestled against my ear while I slept to Aylie's voice on the phone, had exploded like a vibrant fireworks display that occurred just a few months shy of the Fourth of July. The bed was burnt; sheets, pillows, and all. Even though it was horrible, I saw the beauty of God again in that moment before I was rushed to the hospital. The blanket I had bought for grandma just days before her passing had been burned on one spot alone; the edge protecting my face and hair. It was as if grandma had died to be the guardian angel who would save my life from above through that blanket and all of the healing energy that it held.

Two days later, I was doped up due to excruciating pain and wheel-chair-bound on a plane headed for California, where I would begin yet another chapter of my life.

# Chapter 15

# Things Go From Bad to Worse

## Interlude 5: Back to Aylie

My relationship with Aylie came at quite a cost. While I became the self-employed co-owner of MEB, a direct-mail home improvement advertising magazine in L.A. County, drove a brand-new leased car with a souped-up subwoofer system, bright yellow paint, and black tinted windows, which I affectionately named "Bumblebee," had season tickets to the WNBA, ate fine cuisine on an almost nightly basis, went on mini-vacations at least once a month, and lived the good life, that deck of cards inevitably came crashing down. Throughout the course of our relationship, Aylie became painfully addicted to liquid Vicodin, and after years as a suffering enabler, having given her an ultimatum, "it is either go to rehab or lose me," she chose both. Here again, I was brought into a woman's life just to fix their problems and leave. With nowhere to go and no one to turn to, I placed my faltering trust in the hands of an old friend—a felon and self-proclaimed con-artist—under the foolish belief that she had changed.

## Love is: Making Stupid Mistakes in a Blind

Devastated and alone, I crumbled. I had been avoiding Jen for a while until Aylie went into rehab, and Jen and I started talking again, moderately. Meanwhile, I was being physically pushed out of Aylie's home after a solid promise that she would never kick me out without a place to stay—and I felt utterly destroyed. One evening, I received an all-too perfectly timed phone call from my old junior high school friend Erin. She suggested that I move to Pennsylvania with her and her happily employed husband and her precious young children until I could figure it all out. So that is what I did. I walked out of my fairy tale and into a modern-day nightmare.

A lot of things went into that decision. In retrospect, Jen told me I had always had a home with her, but I didn't truly see it. If I had, I wonder if I would have even taken it. She was with her girlfriend Cynthia in Virginia at the time and even if I had found my way there, I would feel the constant piercing of daggers in my heart to see her with another woman that she loved, as she loved Cynthia. Instead, I took the word of a not-so-good person who had been my best friend before the time of Jen, had endured my adolescent suffering throughout high school, and whom I had been intimate with sexually on several occasions. That is why I moved myself and all of my belongings across the entire country from the California coastline to the Pennsylvania suburbs. I would later hear this same woman speak the words "I have been through a lot. That is why I am now homicidal rather than suicidal"—the threat echoing through my head as I ran to the other side of the state to get away from her and her new husband, and, more importantly, myself.

## Interlude 6: The Spaces in Between

It's always in the past that the present makes sense. Jen may have never known it, but when she shut me out in Florida and began to sleep with practically every girl in the old skool crew that she had amassed, it made me run into the arms of every man that I could find. I couldn't bring myself to be in a relationship with another woman until years later, so, eventually I pacified my time with other members of her friend circle—namely, her distant cousin: the same cousin that I would later find myself in an orgy with, and whom would take my female virginity in the same night, along with a pizza delivery guy, a taxi cab driver, and a "girl" now known on the street as Molly. I would also go on to date a straight girl named Michelle whom I never actually slept with, and about seventy men that I did not care about at all, with whom I did.

Back in the day, I had an uncanny and completely unintentional habit of sleeping with Erin's boyfriends. Among those men were a) the guy who seduced me in the pool at my apartment and who ended up being Erin's husband, unbeknownst to me;  b) the boy James that I mentioned before, who I slept with behind the store during my high school years, and proceeded to huff gasoline with for a few months after, and c) the strange country boy named Jeremy who I knew from junior high school, and who also ended up dating Erin.  Of the latter, let me explain:

I was out partying at Club Energy when I walked into the abandoned building next door to get some air and found Jeremy doing some nighttime construction. After a few minutes of conversation in my inebriated state, I found myself ripping off Jeremy's toolbelt while he sucked on my neck and earlobe. We ended up fucking on the new countertop of a torn-down bathroom, which, ironically, was so dirty with sawdust and metal scraps that it was oddly sexy.  In that installment of our friendship, Erin tried to convince me constantly to be with a man instead of pining after a woman. Pining after Jen. She knew me too well. Well, what can I say...mission accomplished?

Erin and I ended up having our own hookups, the first one being after a girl's night out playing pool and drinking beer at a local dive bar on the river. We spent endless hours building upon a growing sexual tension with both our words and our body language and showing off our pool playing skills with an air of feminine bravado. Out of nowhere, we would find ourselves slammed against the wall of a bathroom stall making out (see, it all starts with bodies slamming against walls), to a bed, to having sex with her and a friend named Jean Paul, to the floor of Jeremy's apartment, to Sandy and I fooling around with her at her trailer—each time so messed up that I can barely remember how I wound up there in the first place.

Did I mention that I also ended up sleeping with this guy named Frankie during a super intense acid trip? The same man who she was yet to know and who would later become her husband as well.

# Suicide Missions

So...I flew across the country from California to Pennsylvania. I even shipped my cat, Latte, whom I would lose, along with my life possessions and my last physical memories of grandma, including the couch she slept on every night, that I could not bear to part with and the hope chest that her great grandmother gave her, along with the painting of cows that my great great grandmother made, given to me by a family friend.

I started out the first night, curled up with my two past lovers, just cuddling with a bottle of Sailor Jerry and getting smoked out. The next day, while Erin was gone on errands, Frankie and I became close again. Too close. He was cuddling with me and began to rub my breasts and kiss my neck, and then ran his hands along my tummy and began to kiss it...I had not been with a man in over five years, and I was certainly not going to be with Erin's now- husband, with or without her permission. I panicked and I stopped him. That's when things took a shift for the worse. I remember Frankie started talking about a bone saw he had. I remember a video they had me watch on Crips vs. Blood gangs, and when they closed up an open area downstairs with a fan, I thought they were trapping me in and poisoning me. Then when Frankie cooked for me but no one else ate it, I thought the same. They started talking about people dying in jail of broken glass in their food. I heard discussions about actually killing people and I started hiding out in my room; my small, half-bath sized room was stuffed with an apartment's worth of furniture, and my cat, who could not dare leave the room as she would be eaten by the large pit bull in the living room, was terrified.

Then the two of them started to leave me alone, more and more, to babysit her three children. I felt trapped like a caged rat. I had moved up there under the promise that they had two cars, a job, and a good life and home, and simply wanted me to have a place to come to relax until I could figure it all out again. I figured I could help them with their bills and be an effective friend to them. What I became was their next con.

This banter of death and mayhem went on for days, until I finally overheard Erin one day say, "give her three days and then kill her." I panicked. I started praying like I had never prayed before. I listened to Christian music blaring from my Ipod headphones as I started to run through all the dark areas of my mind to figure out what they were planning, always striving to be one step ahead. I started to make plans, pack bags, and slowly worked my way out.

On that fateful third day, I walked down the stairs at eight in the morning, just to see Frankie wide awake, relaxing on my grandmother's couch. He saw the red suitcase I was rolling behind me and asked me "are you going on a trip?"

I responded nonchalantly. "I'm going to look for work and I wanna do some things but I need some stuff with me." I had packed everything I couldn't part with except furniture, my cat, and my musical equipment. But at this moment, none of that mattered. I just wanted to get out of there alive.

He responded with the cunning of a fox. "You probably shouldn't take that much with you or you might get stopped by the cops for being homeless and get locked up."

I went upstairs and purged myself of everything but the absolute essentials, and, with two days-worth of clothes on my body, went back downstairs, out the door, and out of their lives, forever. I walked almost thirty miles that day, in directions I didn't know, starting with a walk to an unknown park where I would get down on my hands and knees and beg God to give me direction. I took a few rides from strangers, telling them bits and pieces of my story, and having angels watch over me as I traveled towards safety. I went into a Salvation Army station where a nice lady gave me bus fare to make it to the airport, over an hour away. I called Aylie and told her what had happened. As I stood with the phone at my ear, I pleaded with her. "If you ever loved me, even for a moment, you will get me a ticket back to California and save my life."

#TheHeartWantsWhatItWants

# Chapter 16

## Embracing Life Again

### Getting Back on God's Path

Aylie picked me up from the airport at six the next night. As I walked into the terminal, my memory of deep embraces after being away from her in the past was replaced by nothing more than the cold gesture of a pat on the back. I drug myself to her car, with only the four layers of clothing on my back, a bag of writing journals, and an IPod.

I spent the next few months couch surfing at Aylie's house, with what was left of us completely shattered. The upside to this decision is that my journey after Aylie continued onward into a four-year university stint at California State.

I guess in retrospect, my grandma had to lose her life so I could live mine. Regardless, some trades are not worth making. I continued my bachelor's degree, brought my GPA up, and eventually started student teaching for my dual-enrollment bachelors and credential.

That is when I met Jerri.

## JERRI

I was online, this time not caring about talking or relationships. I just wanted to fuck. I just wanted to take myself out of the hell I had been in and have cybersex, safe and non-committal, with women across the world. No strings. Ships passing in the night. I did this with about four women, finding that "no strings attached" was an unrealistic concept, even in a fantasy world. I met one girl from the UK who started to cling quite quickly. Another had an obsession with the movie "Loving Annabelle" and wanted to role-play the characters from the movie again and again and again: 'Next!' There was one woman who just needed someone, and I was ok with that. Roseanne. She just needed someone to love her. I was okay pretending to be that person for a brief instant, but when she invited me to come live with her and her kids, I knew it was time to stop playing games. Then, while I was chatting with the pseudo-friends I had made online, I ran into Jerri. We talked. For hours. Eventually she showed me a picture of her, and <u>only</u> her. She was cute!

I started to really like her; not love. Not that soon. On her birthday, I called her and had phone sex with her while Jeremih's "Birthday Sex" played in the background. As I finished repeatedly coming, and going again, and again, I physically fell off the couch. A few weeks later, when I would slip down the staircase while hearing her say "I love you" for the first time, we would joke for years to come that that was the moment I literally *fell* in love with her. We had an adorable first date. Since she lived in Texas, I pieced together pictures of things I wanted to do with her. Dinners. Trips. Life. I put them together in a slide show and we pretended we were doing all those things. It was an awesome virtual date.

After a month, I decided to go meet her and figure out what this was. I wasn't throwing around the major "I love you" yet, but I did tell her I thought I was falling for her. I flew out to visit her and we had our first soft kiss hours after I landed, when we were taking a ferry over to Galveston, Texas to go swimming in the Gulf of Mexico.

It was gentle. It was innocent. It was everything I missed about women. Not since Hannah had I really been courted or wooed. I had been lusted after, fucked stupid and sucked ravishingly, wined and dined endlessly, but I missed this. The real essence of falling in love, set to the backdrop of what would later become our song, and said everything she had to say: Billy Currington's "Must Be Doing Something Right."

Even though I could have given "it" to her as we made out in the ocean in the following hours after, I reserved myself this time. I didn't want to sleep with her.

Not yet.

I was learning about myself all over again.

## Interlude 7: Reflections

After some serious soul searching, I realized that the only women that I could not sleep with right away were the ones I had real feelings for. That difference left me reserved and virgin-like, and I shied away at second base, like I had with many women before, but it wasn't awkward with her. It was natural. It was the moment.

Next, we traveled to Canyon Country to stay at her timeshare. I spent the day getting to know her even better and feeling so connected to her that I didn't need to rush anything. It was late night, about three in the morning, and we were lying in bed together. I looked over at her, butterflies in my stomach, and decided to step out on the balcony and smoke a cigarette. Little did I know, I would spend hours on that deck, going through a half pack of smokes, trying to decide if I wanted to give myself away again, this time to a woman who I felt so comfortable with and in tune with that I didn't *have* to do anything at all.

I gathered my courage as the sun was just starting to rise. I walked into the bedroom, slid on top of her slowly, and kissed her deeply, before removing her clothes, and her removing mine. A few hours later, I woke up, wrapped in her arms, around her naked body, a sense of peace and pride consuming me. I didn't think that after everything, the flame of Jen that I to this day couldn't extinguish, the pain of Erin and her ultimate betrayal, and the sting of Aylie's cold and changing heart, that I would ever feel what it was like to love anyone or anything again. But it was this morning that I realized that I had found the woman I wanted to be with in this new chapter of my life.

When I left at the end of the week, we were closer than we had ever been. We exchanged the words "I love you" and were trying to make the long-distance work. By the end of the year, she was making plans to move out to California to be with me. This was a change of pace. Up until this point, I had always moved for my women. But I was steadfast on finishing my Bachelor's degree, and she decided that she didn't want to wait any longer to be a physical part of my daily life. Our life.

Within six months, she had moved out to California with me to start that life together. Little did we know the turns that our life would take. Like all of the other moments in my life so far, one of the most significant twists came in the form of a woman.

## The Dastardly Temptations of Dragon Mcfirepants

In true nature, I am a monogamous spirit and I seem to mate for life. This is tragic, however, when the mating of my soul happened many decades ago, yet the actual mating of my body to that body had never happened at all. I would later find that this made me question my own sense of monogamy. How could I love two women in such totally different ways, but be committed to both?

Even though one of these women was barely in my life anymore, I would dream about her, call her every so often, just to hear her answering machine. I still didn't understand this, so I dabbled in the experiments of other women. It happened like this again and again, during the first few years of Jerri and I's relationship. I would be tempted endlessly by women whom I would try to only give affection to in Jerri's presence, and only after long discussions of pretenses and intentionality. The truth is that I have never been good at fighting off a beautiful woman's advances, but I have become quite good at stopping them before it goes too far. So goes the story of Dragon McFirepants.

*In the writing of this section, I called "her" to ask permission to share our trysts in these pages. She agreed to this under the stipulation that, due to her married status, I would use an alias. She chose Dragon McFirepants of her own volition. I agreed.*

I met Dragon at a house party that some friends of mine were invited to. When I first looked at her, I saw a spark in her eyes which proceeded to melt me like a flame. We hit it off very quickly, our passion fueled by women's intuition and cheap whiskey. It was she who came on to me first though, as I wouldn't cross the boundary of her matrimony... not just yet anyways.

I would love to say that this started off slowly, but that would be a lie. It started off like a race car, revving my engine before the first flag was waved. Dragon started by picking my poison and refilling my shot glass every fifteen minutes. She kissed me at first quickly, while her husband had left the room. Then, a few minutes later, she followed me into the bathroom and pushed me against the door, my hands clasped above us, our mouths, searching for one another, on this seemingly uneventful night, and this was the M.O. of many nights to come.

I was at Dragon's house on one particular night, about to pass out with Jerri on the living room floor. As I curled up and began to kiss Jerri, Dragon returned from her bedroom, fumbling around in the dark, and moved herself on top of us both. She began grinding herself into the blanket that separated us, straddling both Jerri and I's legs, and kissing us. I knew Jerri didn't know what to make of this by the way that she shied away, but I was so turned on, I kissed Dragon back. Feverishly. At once, I was overtaken with lust and pulled Dragon more directly against me. Our bodies crashed into each other for several minutes, but as I held back a moan and reached out for Jerri's hand, she buried her head in the crevice of my neck. Feeling concerned that I was crossing an impenetrable line, I stopped gyrating against Dragon, leaned against my side, and felt her intended kiss graze my cheek as she whisked herself away like a breeze that had changed directions, like a phantom, disappearing into the night.

I would love to say that it stopped there, but it didn't. Anytime we were in each other's presence, Dragon and I couldn't keep our hands or lips off of each other. We would wait, not so patiently, for her husband to go do something, anything, and then we would be all over each other like cheap rugs. It was like this for almost a year, finding little nooks and crannies to make out in, groping, ripping off clothes, always going just so far, at the edge of the blade, but just right at the verge of not being able to take it back. I should have seen what was truly happening the night that I called her name and she said back to me, in the most sultry and seductive voice, "Just call me Beelzebub." I was terrified by her and yet so turned on. She was violently tender and set my sex on fire. But this is what happens when an angel and a demon collide. I will leave it up to you to say which is which.

Jerri began to set limits. I could only go over to Dragon's house if Jerri was there. Alright. Let's hit the bar!

One of the worst things that came out of our little rendezvous was the realization that her relationship with her husband was taking a turn for the worst. He became verbally and physically abusive. She would walk into a million doorknobs that year, fall from flightless stairs, and Jerri and I began to seriously consider helping her out of all this. She called one night, asking for us to come over between sobs. We showed up to her house and the place had been ransacked. The living room coffee table was flipped over, broken to pieces, and things were strewn everywhere. Dragon was just sitting with this wild expression on her face in the middle of the floor, with a bottle of whiskey and three shot glasses.

That night she told me about her best friend knowing about this "side" of her husband, and she told me a code word that they shared if things went too far. Jerri and I discussed having her move in with us if things got that bad. All I could think to myself was 'Oh great, another three-way relationship, because the last one ended so well.' Meanwhile, I felt myself getting closer and closer to mistaking lust for love.

The night that really defined us was yet to come. It was during one of our usual drinking nights, where we first went to the bar and then ended up in Dragon's bed. It was like any other night at our local dive bar; I was wearing my new Rolling Stone T-Shirt, showcasing the lyrics of Marvin Gaye's "What's Going On." Dragon handed me a shot and as I sipped down the devil's nectar, she proceeded to start to slip my shirt over my head; fearing she was leaving me half naked in the middle of the bar, Dragon grabbed my hand and led me to the bathroom, pushing me into a stall, running her hands between my thighs, and put the shirt on herself, claiming it as hers. But she wouldn't give me her shirt in return. So, Jerri and I went out to the car and grabbed one of her button up shirts, and we decided to leave the bar and head back to Dragon's house.

When we arrived, Dragon again avoided her husband by following me into the bathroom. All of a sudden, she starts grabbing my tits, throws my body up on the sink and starts biting my neck, as usual. As we slam up against the wall again, all hot and bothered, I can see that look in her eye. She's not done. She ushers me into her bedroom, throws me down on the bed, and we start going at it, as Jim Morrison might say, like *"children, soft driven, slow and mad, like some new language/reaching your head with the cold, sudden fury of a divine messenger/let me tell you about heartache and the loss of god/ wandering, wandering in hopeless night"* (The Doors, "Stoned Immaculate"). I call Jerri in to join us. She comes in and closes the door and as they kiss for a second, things start to get real. Jerri lays down on the bed, rubbing her leg against me, her hands roaming, and as I pull off her shirt, Dragon finally has me for the first time, down to my underwear. While we are both kissing and touching, each one working down a side of Jerri, I take one look at Jerri, see that she has a mixed expression of turned-on and hurt, and proceed to reach down in a half-stupor, and pull my jeans back on, breathless. Dragon leaves the room. Thinking I have done the right thing, I go to hold Jerri, but all she tells me is that I gave her female blue balls. Fucking women!

Dragon and I do not speak very often. On one drunken occasion, I told her I was falling for her, which put the nail in the proverbial coffin of our affair, as it rightfully needed to. But I can never forget her and as I have seen in years of late, she will never let me. We text each other a few times a year, just letting the other know that the friendship was there even after the glitter faded. But nothing lasts forever.

# Winning The Battle. But Losing The War

**To my best friend Sasha:**

Like many other sacred people in my life, Sasha was not long for this world. She left it on October 11, 2011. An overdose. A homicide... They are one in the same in pill-mill Florida. Sasha had always suffered back pain from the time that she lifted a box working in her teens and pulled her sciatic nerve. Her back transformed into a shamble of slipped discs and pinched nerves. While her life progressed into an endless routine of pains and pills, she was still the one person who would pull me out of the rubble after my grandma's death and now she, too, was up in heaven with her.

I received the call on my way to class, wearing my lucky testing charm, my green Element t-shirt with a hole in the left corner and fabric thinning out from years of wear and wash. While standing, I received the call. Within an instant, I was on the bed, crying. We stayed in close touch with each other when I left Florida. I called my professor to ask for a makeup day, but there was no response. I pretended, then, that I was okay; I pretended that I was not metaphorically walking on sharp glass with every step that I took outside my door, every mile that I, barreled over in emotional pain, experienced on the car ride to school. As Jerri drove me to my exam, I was completely incapable of motion, surviving solely on autopilot shock.

Sasha was a fighter. She was capable of motion even in agonizing pain. I loved her from the bottom of my heart. She was the one female friend who was sexually attracted to women that I didn't have sex with. I didn't want to. I saw her as a sister. She held love in her heart for a boy who shall not be named out of reverence for her privacy. I spent many an hour talking to her about her own issues of unrequited love, and I knew her emotional pain because it was my own.

*To Sasha: I love you sis. I will see you soon. But not too soon. I have too much work to do here; souls to save and words to carve in stone. Know that you will be immortalized, both in my memory and my pages. I will always be with you.*

Now let's go get fucked up.

# Chapter 17

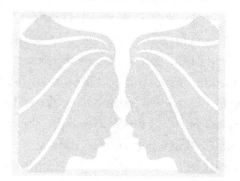

# Getting By, By Getting High

## More Rave Madness

These stories are mixed up. So what? I can do that. I can write about the *after* during the *before*. Catharsis, it seems, can come from the rendering of the story without relying on a timeline. Many years ago, we walked into the club together —the night that Jen told a stranger I was her girlfriend. The fact that it was a tactic employed to brush off unwanted attention didn't matter to me. In this statement, the world was as it should be. I took her hand and walked her into, and quickly out of, a sea of people. As the Jawbreaker ecstasy pills kicked in, I found myself in a courtyard, barely able to move, leaning against her, wrapped in her arms. I kissed her, as I always do, for simple brief moments, but all we have in life are moments. I felt at total peace just wrapped in her embrace. As she began massaging my shoulders, I melted like Jello. I stood up while the room was spinning and nodded out next to her on an almost-too-intense high. When I came to, I asked Jen to share a moment with me. I sat in front of her, my legs crossed indian-style, and she responded in kind. As I gazed into her beautiful eyes, I told her I would give her any part of me that she wanted. I can't remember exactly what she said. I believe she may have asked for my "luck." But I gave it to her. She said she wanted to give me any part of her that I wanted. I told her I wanted part of her "charm." She gave that to me. We felt the exchange like electricity through our bodies, as if the world opened up to another reality—one that allowed this type of thing. This was not the world others know about; it was a world only we knew existed. The rest of the night blurs itself in that magical moment when our essences danced together, mixing heart-parts with soul-parts. As Shakespeare once said in *The Tempest*: "This is the stuff that dreams are made of."

Then there was the night when Jen and her girlfriend Rita invited me to a house party. Jen was exceptionally needy that night. She wanted her girlfriend to believe that she was rolling when, in fact, she was stone cold sober. I was only made aware of this when she leaned over and whispered it into my ear. However, when she overacted and seemed to be desperately in need of water, some asshole came over with ice and started ramming it down her throat. I took it as a metaphorical assault. The way he jammed the ice cubes in her mouth was violently sexual, and I began to slip into a state of aggression, the likes of which I had never seen in myself before. We went upstairs. Jen laid out on the floor and I cuddled with her. Leaning over her body, laying against her stomach, kissing her again and yet again—another self-compromising position I placed myself in. I knew her girlfriend would be coming back from an errand soon. I reached for the ashtray with marijuana in it and proceeded to flush the household stash, ashtray and all.

We laughed like little school children. My rage intensified. In a cloud of red, I proceeded to break up the rest of the house, ripping VHS tapes apart, dumping spices all over the floor. It was only when I reached for a barbell upon which I had set my sights on throwing through their glass doors that Jen reminded me with an eye wink of the act that she was putting on, and luckily, I relented.

I felt a need to protect her that night, even though I am not so good at guarding myself. As our night drew to a close, the homeowners begged us to leave. We caught up with Rita outside and Jen kicked the acting up a notch. She sprawled out on the backseat of Rita's car, winking intermittently at me, her secret safe inside the haloed chambers of my stoned walls—barren from the act of released aggression.

# Chapter 18

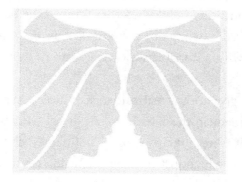

# What it Really Takes to Change the World

## Little Shop of Junior High Horrors

At this point, I'd also been through over five years of college-based educational instruction and three hundred community service hours doing observations and teacher aide work in schools throughout the country. I knew High School was my desired teaching track, but my credentialing program required one semester of Junior High and one semester of High School student teaching. I decided that I would get Junior High out of the way. I threw on some professional clothes, built the ten-page plus lesson plans that I was taught in college were, as my professors deemed them, "presentation worthy", and armed with this and the notion of truly being great, I walked into the classroom. What happened next, however, I was not prepared for. My master teacher tells me that I am so good, I can start teaching the class myself in the first week, even though she is supposed to model what to do for the first month. It is here that I submit. I'm hungry. Fresh blood. "Feed me Semour," (*Little Shop of Horrors, -Musical*).

I spent the next few months working every day with the class, teaching lesson after lesson, all the while being told I was doing a great job by my master teacher. Then, however, came the shock of a lifetime. I was supposed to have a College supervisor observe me— she had been missing in action for the last two months. Finally, when they scraped the bottom of the barrel to make sure my credentialing did not end up out of compliance with state rules, I ended up with a horrible supervisor who told me I was doing it all wrong.

She would not give me any real guidance or direction but she questioned every move that I made in the classroom. At first, I truly tried to change the things that she felt were not up to par. I condensed the size of my lesson plans at her request, which just became confusing for me, and I attempted to model the same things that I was seeing in the classroom, from what I now know was also a horrible mentor teacher. She would berate her students when they misbehaved rather than correct the behavior. She would teach very little and expected them to do even less. One day they were writing letters to Santa; on another, they were simply listening to her read a story to them. I felt like I was drowning with no real guidance, and then the true death blow came down. I had been recommended for improvement, meaning that I would not be signed off as having completed the Junior High portion of my student teaching yet, and only had four more weeks of instruction before they would make their final decision.

Around this time, I also found myself slipping up in the pronoun game, you know, the game you play when you don't want someone to know that you are gay? It's the game you play when someone asks how the person you are involved with is, and it goes somewhat like this:

"**We** are very happy... **The two of us** went to dinner the other night and **we** had a splendid time... **They** are the best thing that has happened in my life..." etcetera, etcetera.

While discussing the idea of having coffee with my partner and my "mentor", I responded "I'll ask *her*," and I immediately felt the scornful eyes of my master teacher glaring back at me with overtly-religious judgment.

I knew at that moment that I had messed up. Royally. By being myself, I became what she could not fathom: a future *lesbian* teacher.

The day I received an unsatisfactory report and was denied the ability to continue through the Junior High portion of my student teaching was one of the saddest days of my life. I spent three hours discussing this via phone with both the mentor and the supervisor. Even though they both wrote reports about my inability to teach, the mentor told me that she alone would have passed me, proving that instead of having my back, she simply ran me under the bus. It took the efforts of many friends in college and Jerri to finally make me realize that I was an awesome teacher and that these people were just dinosaurs who were on their way out of the teaching profession because they were falling so quickly behind the times. I even spoke to my previous teaching instructors about the incident, and they said unofficially that I "was special and would make a difference, and that threatened the old system of teaching to the point that they could not understand me". But they also reminded me that my instructors did understand me and that I would "go on to do great things."

This is exactly what it took for me to move on and graduate with my English degree so that I could finally become a real teacher in a different state.

## Genevi The Great

This was, however, not before meeting the teaching mentor who truly gave me the wings to fly. Genevi was a beautiful soul whom I met through a chance encounter. While doing some basic required hours of observation at a high school in California, the teacher whom I was observing told me that it would benefit me to go see her old student teacher who had become a Pre-AP teacher. I decided to stop by Genevi's classroom in passing, just to see what it was that the other teacher wanted me to see. We hit it off immediately. She, sensing I was an intelligent student teacher who truly wished to start teaching, and I, thinking she was positively stunning, both as a teacher and a woman. I could be very happy spending time in her classroom!

We planned on meeting for sushi in Pasadena that weekend to work out the details of an unofficial student-teacher relationship.

It was a quiet Sunday morning, roasting in the California sun. Jerri drove me to the location that Genevi and I had settled on, but as I thought back to the blackballing I had received at the previous school (a dismissal that I believe to this day was partly in due to my unintentional disclosure of my sexual orientation) I decided to ask Jerri to stay in the car during our luncheon. As I sat with Genevi eating sushi, I began to feel comfortable enough to disclose my sexuality. I told her all of it. I told her I was gay and that I believed part of the reason I did not get a satisfactory report at the Junior High School had to do with this fact. She completely dismissed my anxiousness, instead insisting that I go get Jerri right that instant. She would proceed to scold me incessantly for leaving Jerri in the hot car for almost an hour and repeatedly asked me if she looked like someone who would be that judgmental or bigoted. I was mortified. It seemed that the very closet that the Junior High School wanted me in was the open door that Genevi wanted me out of. To some degree, I believe she might have even liked Jerri more than me, as she continuously threatened in a playful way, "...if you are not careful, I'm going to steal Jerri away from you!"

On that note, we proceeded to hang out as friends, sharing shopping trips and dinners and spending time getting to know each other while I came every other week to the school and taught her tenth grade Pre-AP class. This is about the time when I truly fell in love with the idea of being a Gifted and Advanced Placement teacher.

Genevi's openly acceptant attitude towards me being a lesbian and a teacher made a very deep impression on me. She lived in Long Beach in what she called the "gayborhood" because of the predominance of its openly homosexual population. She spoke quite frequently about my sexuality, my plans of building a life with Jerri, and even of my own presence as a beautiful gay woman. I quickly developed a crush on my mentor, wondering if she might be into me a little too. The answer to that question came in the form of David, the man whom she has now been happily married to for many years. Regardless of this, I consider Genevi a dear friend that I have made during my travels, and I feel truly blessed having known her and having become a better person (and teacher) for it.

## Juggling a Woman and A Career

There is an age-old adage that comes from the discourse of Murphy's Law: "anything that can go wrong... will go wrong." Now no one knows this better than I. I started out in the teaching force, ready to change the world and create a better tomorrow; I wanted to fill the world with hope, culture, and substance, for so many youths are deficient in any (or all) of the above. In the famous words of Wu-Tang Clan's RZA, *"There isn't a chance for the physically dead, but there is still a chance for the mentally dead"* (Gravediggaz, "Twelve Jewels"). That was my purpose: to awaken young minds. That is the calling that God had put upon me.

When I left the pro-bono position with my APs, they all chose to sign my graduation cap for my Bachelors. I still have that cap; it serves as a constant reminder of the impact that I make in the teaching world, and I treasure it still to this day.

## Riding the Wave Towards a Tsunami

I dealt with a lot of things during my first few years teaching on my own, though. I had chosen to work with at-risk youth at a Public Charter School because I wanted to make a difference and I felt that the principal of the school had the same thing in mind. I also had amazing kids; I loved my job and the ninety-nine percent that were amazing and receptive, as was evident from the yearbook that they plastered with messages of love and good will at the end of my first year. In my short time there, I helped a few students choose to stay in school, and a few more got into good colleges. But one situation brought me to my knees, and once again had me running for my life.

One day, a student who had been a bit of a trouble-maker wrote a threat on a paper he turned in, declaring that "snitches catch a red beam", which was referencing the time earlier that week when I caught him in the bathroom causing trouble with his buddies. He would draw gang signs on his work and folders, and this was the real deal. I had never dealt with this level of evil before; I didn't feel safe after that and I didn't feel like I was getting any support from my administration. I left the school on a psychological medical leave and never turned back. It took three months of counseling and a new city to help me move beyond the horrible reality of my recent teaching past; all the while, a voice echoing in my mind, "try as you might, you can't save them all."

# Chapter 19

# True Love Comes Back Around

## New Chapters and Old Stories

It's funny how people try to figure out what I believe with all my heart exists of *true love*; how they attempt to make it fit some preconceived notion of what it is supposed to look like. Devoted. Domesticated. Simple. So much so, that when it sits right in front of them, the attempt to explain it negates the very love itself and lessens its worth. This is the new lesson I was learning from Jen.

Our interaction with one another slowed down for quite a while. When the relationship with Jerri began, Jen and I were just texting every so often; a call or two here and there. Mainly reminiscing about our past because our future was so unclear. It was at the beginning of 2014 that our unofficial love affair began to take wings again and fly once more.

It was around June of this year when I started to see *her* lovelight again too. It started with over twelve hundred miles of distance; me at home, her at a karaoke bar. The phone call started with the cliché' words "I Heart You." Seemingly insignificant slang until what it signified spoke all the words that Jen never could. And then Jen took the stage to sing, with me listening to her voice croon Hall and Oates's "Sara Smile" into the phone. As the song ended, she proceeded to ask me to do something: to watch "Orange is the New Black" on Netflix; more specifically, one episode where those words were used. I asked her if I should watch it with Jerri, and her response at first was that it would be okay, but then she censored this answer and responded, "No. Watch it alone." In this episode, two lesbians, tragically fated to be in jail with one another, lie in each other's arms in a quiet moment, gazing into each other's eyes, and one says, "I Heart You" to the other. Then the other responds "I heart you, is that I love you for pussies?" (OITNB, "Tall Men With Feelings" 2013).

There is a high significance in the meaning of the words "I Heart You": it is usually said by those who cannot get truly in touch with their feelings but know what it is that they feel, even if they suck at expressing it. And the jail? Was that a real prison made of bars or the place where we found ourselves trapped together, clinging to each other out of a love that could never be denounced or defined?

At that moment, I felt the answer to my question of where we were with each other now, almost twenty years later, hit me like a ton of bricks: *She's still in love with me too.* There's a funny thing that occurs when you reach an epiphany that your heart has been holding back; that every moment that you try to deny how you feel actually makes what you feel grow even stronger. Those three little words meant even more than "I love you"—words that get thrown around too much. Jen had found a symbiosis with these two star-crossed lovers who are destined to be, comparing them directly to us. She was letting the show talk for her, and that is the precise moment that I lost my own fight against letting myself love her all over again.

I proceeded to watch the entire series, noting that we were just like these two women, who were madly in love. The one did not treat the other very well, but the other was far from innocent. They had a falling out. The one girl had another lover. All the pieces fit. Some of the lines from the show were actual things that we had said, at some point over the last twenty years, to one another. It felt as if we were Piper and Alex, two women who could not deny the love they shared but somehow always missed the opportunity to stay committed to one another. Just like Chicago says, *"Two hearts drawn together, bound by destiny"* (Chicago, "Will You Still Love Me?").

Life, however, is a balancing act. You can't really have the good without the bad. It was at this point in my life that I would also suffer the most severe injury I had ever gone through—one that would require major surgery and seemingly endless months to heal.

## The Path from Health is Paved with Good Intentions

I spent the early part of July in the hospital and the rest of the year in a wheelchair. Here's how it all "went down" (pardon the ridiculous pun): while working with a personal trainer on getting into shape, Jerri and I took bi-daily turns doing cardio and aerobic exercise routines at the local gym. On the day in question, we were both doing stair lifts on a massive tire. About halfway in, I noticed myself feeling fatigued and dizzy. I decided that this was a sign of weakness, rather than a warning of impending doom. I chose to be a trooper and continue my exercise routine. As I stepped down from number sixteen of my twenty reps, my right ankle buckled and I fell to the ground. The excruciating pain that followed was a combination of the starting fracture of my foot from the fall, and a subsequent triple fracture caused by the dislocation of my ankle, which sent my foot coasting into a metal rack. As the EMTs lifted my body onto a stretcher, I knew I was in trouble. And as I went under the knife, the last person I thought about, that I needed to help pull me through, was Jen.

When I was a child, I had a premonition that I would end up in a wheelchair by the time I was 40. At first, I believed that this would be due to the unexplainable fore-mentioned injuries that my body sustained as an infant. Life, as it turns out, is not without a sense of irony. Instead of being a result of my unhealthy beginning, this injury was a result of my attempt at being the healthiest I have been in my entire life. I would spend the next six months teaching high school from a wheelchair. This was an amazing and terrifying experience, all at the same time. On the one hand, the children were great. They pushed my wheelchair around the campus and genuinely took it easy on me, for the most part. On the other hand, a few troublemakers took this opportunity to try to get away with everything in the book, as my ability to thwart disruptive behavior was hindered by an obvious inability to correct behaviors quickly that were going on behind me. As a result, I spent most of my teaching days rolling around for hours on end, trying to gain a bird's eye view of my classroom from constantly shifting vantage points. In the end, this made me a stronger teacher, but I went through hell to get back to where I am today, and, for a while, I didn't believe I would ever walk again.

Jerri and I also lost our best friend that New Years. Our baby girl Twitch, a beautiful black Labrador with a bit of a mutt mix, ran away from Jerri's parents' house through a damaged wooden door on the gate to their backyard. She came back for just a minute, to say goodbye, and as we put her in the backyard again, I was too tired to remind Jerri that she could get out again unless one of us fixed the hole that aided her escape the last time. Moments later, she was gone for good. Even considering the immense pain that this caused us both, it was one of the best and worst New Years that I have ever had. And it all started with the cliché' words: "Happy New Year".

*EXPRESSING A TWENTY-YEAR LOVE AFFAIR IN FIVE PAGES: THE UPS AND DOWNS OF UNREQUITED REQUITED LOVE*

# Phase One: Reigniting A Flame
# That Never Went Out

At seventeen, I kissed Jen like a tender virgin. During the rave scene, I kissed her numerous times as someone so high that I couldn't remember the feeling, only the moment itself. Each time, I felt like I was kissing a friend. A very high friend. At twenty-five, when she took care of me after a horrible breakup, her kiss was comforting and sweet; romantic. Now, at thirty-six, when I was to kiss her again, I did not know what to expect.

Drunk, passionate, slightly violent, slamming each other against walls. Sounding like the beginning of many of my now infamous relationships with women. But I will explain this later.

If "I Heart You" was our turning point, then New Years became the point of no return. After six months of listening to love songs the way we used to, letting the lyrics say the things we couldn't, and after asking her to be the Maid of Honor at Jerri and I's wedding (of which I will expound later), Jen and I's relationship began to take another turn. Through songs like Jason Aldean's "Do You Wish It Was Me," and Kenny Roger's "Lady," she continually prodded into my soul, always asking me to listen specifically to the lyrics and to know they were meant from her and for me; making me question how deep our roots went—if I could marry Jerri while being in love with her, and if I could ever live without Jen's love again. All the while, noncommittal; refusing to step up and tell me exactly how she felt. Until New Years, when all her playing-hard-to-get came to an end, and the card deck that we had systematically reshuffled had been brought to bear; laid out on the table to be "weighed and measured." But, just as in a *Knight's Tale*, would it be "found lacking?"

I told Jerri that I wanted to talk to Jen for New Year's Eve. She understood. She always understands. That's why, when I ran upstairs to toast in the new year on Skype, Jerri drifted to sleep downstairs on her parent's couch in Texas. It was only after a few shots of Christian Brothers Brandy that the night took on a mind of its own. This simple drunken Skype session, one the likes of endless nights in many months' past, turned into a picturesque slide from the movie of my life. At one point, I found myself feeling like Cary Grant in an old black and white movie; an iconic scene in which I literally stood in the pouring rain, holding onto a metallic light pole during a thunderstorm, screaming into the phone: "But do you love me Jen... Are you in love with me?!" And hearing a resounding response, after a few moments passed, finally breaking the silence-of-my-heart which echoed in her own pause over the phone. "... Okay. Okay! Yes...Yes! I am in love with you Dolores... I guess I always have been."

Her use of my full name, to me, showed her sincerity. My heart fluttered. Time stood still. The world, all at once, became brighter, clearer. In that one moment, I understood all the secrets of the universe. I felt light as air, able to conquer the world. Only one problem remained. How in the world would I tell Jerri?

It was one thing to live in the land of the unknown; part lust, part longing; a fantasy, possibly made from the very air that separated both Jen and I from half a country away. Now, in this moment, when all of my longing ceased, when feelings were being validated and my intuitions proven, the very fabric of my being came to life again—a truth unraveled at the juncture of Jen's lips, and the world took on a completely different hue. I floated into the house in tears; part joy, part anguish. I discussed with Jen how to possibly tell Jerri. Her response: "You're not leaving her. I won't let you." I thought about this for a moment, and quickly took my power back: "I'm not, but please do not think that you have any choice in that matter." I was establishing my facade. I had to. It was the only way I could get through the pain of telling Jerri. And as she cried, I paused my conversation with Jen to console her, ultimately coming to the conclusion that I wasn't going to leave Jerri at all. I was going to convince her that the three of us could work together to figure all this out.

# Chapter 20

# A Dream is a Wish
# Your Heart Makes

## Jerri's Riverwalk Proposal

B ut I digress. I should start back at the beginning. I can do that,
you know. It was the first year that Jerri and I were together,
and after just a few months of our new relationship had passed,
I would find myself in Texas on a pretty regular basis. On one night in particular, we spent a romantic Thanksgiving evening at the several-mile expanse
of restaurants and shopping spaces known as the famous San Antonio Riverwalk. As a standing tradition, the city lit their Christmas tree during a
lavish parade, all in preparation for the impending holiday season. When
we pulled up two chairs that we had snuck into the "reserved" section of the
walk, I felt this strange feeling come over me—I found myself entertaining
the notion that she was going to ask me to marry her.

The entire space went pitch black, as I briefly fantasized about the lights
coming back up—her on one knee, asking me to join her in married bliss—
but when the lights came back on, there she remained, in her chair, just as
she had been before, gently taking my hand in hers, and writing "I Love

You" into the palm of my hand. But when I looked into her eyes, I felt her proposal words too, even though I couldn't hear them.

Not yet.

This was, however, a sign of things to come. Years later, she would tell me that she thought about it at that moment, and when our four-year anniversary rolled around, she told me to be patient—that she would ask me to marry her when she was completely ready. I had never wanted someone to ask me so badly as I did with Jerri. In the past, I had mock proposals to a few girlfriends, but none of these hollow attempts at a marital union stuck.

With Jerri, it was different. I was waiting for her to do it on her own terms.

On the fifth Thanksgiving of our relationship, a month before Jen and I would declare our love mutually for one another, Jerri and I spent the weekend on the same Riverwalk that we began at; this time eating a luxurious afternoon dinner at a restaurant adjacent to the crystal blue river beneath us. I should pause here to mention that, as a child, the lesbian erotica that I had so smut-fully written had ended with a marriage proposal. As part of the serendipity of life, I had already unintentionally lived out several of the chapters of my fantasies after writing them—each experience with a different woman, one by one, throughout many of the latter years of my young adult life. All, that is, but one: getting engaged in a very specific way to marry the woman I love. It all came together with Jerri. Almost to the exact word, Jerri proposed to me much in the same way as my own written prophecies, written oh so long ago in the lesbian erotica novel I wrote in my teens—the one that used to fill Jen, BFLO, and I's nights. It would happen over a lovely dinner, a beautiful hotel room. In this version of the story, she surprised me by sneaking away during our dinner and placing a teddy bear by the bed with a carefully placed note:

*To My Sweet Pea,*
*Like I said before, everything in the right time.*
*I love you so much and cannot wait to spend our lives together.*
*   Love, Your Cuddle Bunny*

When we got back to the room, I quickly noticed her gift. Elated with the note and the teddy bear, it took Jerri prompting me to look at the ribbon closer, as I slowly noticed that the red ribbon around its neck was radiating with light. As I reached towards its shine, I realized that there was something very special attached to its soft fur: a shimmering diamond ring.

And then she got down on one knee. Taking the ring from the teddy bear's ribbon, she gazed into my eyes and placed it on my finger.

"Will you marry me and make me the happiest woman in the world?"

I placed one hand on the bed, holding myself upright as my one-word reply said it all.

"Yes!"

#TheHeartWantsWhatItWants

# Chapter 21

## Journey into Wonderland

### Phase Two: Revisiting Old Feelings with an Old Friend

It was always hard to be away from Jen. For the years that we didn't speak, I thought about her constantly. But after professing our love to each other over New Years, it became virtually impossible to be away from her. I had already planned on visiting her soon, but now I would go on to write these plans in stone. It was over Spring Break later that year that we finally spent time with each other again after re-lived years of endless flirting and searching which led us right up to this moment.

Jerri and I were staying at the beautiful Seascape Motel that we had stayed at the last time that we were in Florida—the same location that I would one day pick as Jerri and I's wedding venue. As soon as we got into town, we stopped at Jen's house, where I proceeded to hold her in our customary much-too-long-to-be-just-friends hug. I held her close, breathing against her neck, smelling her hair. While Jerri unloaded the car, I spent the next few minutes reacquainting myself with Jen's mom and cracking a cold one with Jen while we sat smoking in her backyard. It was almost surreal. I watched her eyes look me completely over from head to toe. I tried to play it cool, but the same butterflies that had captured my teenage heart came fluttering back into the pit of my stomach. Starlight beamed from my eyes, and hers, and I could feel the passionate anticipation close itself into the empty spaces of our all-too-layered conversation. We said our temporary goodbyes as Jerri and I whisked off from her house to the lovers' retreat which the two of us would stay at for most of the nights of our vacation.

I didn't know how far it would go. Two days before, I thought to myself, 'Jen and I have never had timing. It has never felt completely right. She continually told me she didn't feel that way, until the day that she stopped saying that...', and I realized that even though we had always heard love's musical duet, we had never found its lasting rhythm together. But, as I tidied up the room to the motel and got dressed for a night with the two women I loved, I also thought to myself 'Maybe tonight will be the night that we do.'

Jen arrived around six in the afternoon, guitar in-tow. Rocking an old Nirvana t-shirt and jeans, her beauty was so relaxed, so understated. I made myself one of what would become many more whiskey and cokes to come and settled in behind the piano, ready to pour my soul out onto those keys.

The night was epic! We sounded fantastic together. We wrote a little, drank a lot, and flipped through a few cover songs. In a way that bordered on tradition, we found time to step away from the rest of the world and have a deep conversation which, like everyone before it, ended in me professing my love for her. Only this time, instead of trying to let me down easy, which I easily expected her to do, she stepped a little closer to holding her truth. "You are the closest I have ever been to being in love." Those words stabbed my heart. They are at once both beautiful and grotesque. To say this means that she still can't find that place in her heart that will let her let go; let her feel, let her love. I remember too well that she said "I'm in love with you" again this decade, only to take it away before the breath passed her lips.

But this was to be expected. Every woman, every attempt at love, had led her to pain and lies. I have been true in my heart and brave in my honesty. And now I see that she, when she puts that light of hope inside me, is trying to do the same.

*"Women leave impressions on our hearts like handprints. Each one unique. Sometimes the hand is caressing you, other times it is throttling you, but it is permanent regardless."-Dolores*

It went on this way for about twenty minutes until we returned from our heart-to-heart conversation to join our friends. The next thing I remember, amidst more music playing and good times, was a moment that words can't describe. I dropped all my inhibitions and finally mustered my nerve. As she walked out of another room, I stopped her, grabbed her arm gently, and whispered to her "please kiss me." Such a simple request. Expecting her to pacify me with either a gentle rejection or an emotionless kiss, I found myself completely stunned when she pushed me up against the wall and slid her tongue deep in my mouth. Passionate. Raw. I felt a rush of electric shock run through my body, so much so that I threw my cell phone and in this one involuntary act, my nervous system broke the enchantment.

I bit her lip. Hard. Her tongue was huge inside my mouth. Overwhelming. Real. I froze, yet I wanted desperately to walk her through the adjoining bathroom in front of us and fall down onto the bed with her. Moments later, I followed her into that very bathroom and kissed her back. She quickly grabbed me from behind, and wrapped her arms around my waist,-looking in a mirror at our reflection together while playing with Jerri's hair gel. I begged her to spend the night, but she responded that her mom would kill her. Part truth, part cop out. But, as I serenaded her to an impromptu keyboard rendition of "Stroke of Luck" by Garbage, she left me with these words... "Come over and we will spend the night together on Thursday."

I spent the next two days anticipating this. Not like you would think. There's that part of attraction that makes me want to be intimate with her, make love to her, but then this other side, which is the stronger of the two, which is perfectly content just being close and holding her. True love, it seems, has no real agenda. Being super affectionate seemed to have just become our thing. A little window of bliss. Maybe she is just good at giving me what I want, or maybe she feels it too. Once again, I may never know. But I do know that in these moments, these rare occasions where I get to be with her, these are the most intimate things I have ever felt or done with another human being.

It was the awaited Thursday night. Jerri and I showed up to Jen's house in the early evening. There were only two other guests for our bonfire: Jen's niece, and Shane, Jen's close friend. As I sipped on shots and mixed drinks of whiskey, I found myself slowly sliding into a dream world. Every instance, every moment, from a quick kiss on the cheek, to a liturgy of "I Love You's", to the impromptu discussions of sex, I felt the breakdown of my own self unravel; as I danced to Joan Jett by the light of the fire pit, Jen's arms wrapped around my waist. It felt magical. Destined. And then the world went black.

I remember puking my guts up and calling for her. As she sat leaning against the wall in the bathroom, I couldn't help but realize that I was blowing the limited opportunity that I had to spend this time with her. I crashed out in the air mattress Jerri and I were sleeping on, and the night went on without me.

Looking back, Jerri said that the silence in my absence from the fire pit was deafening. Crickets. I came to, regaining consciousness, with Jerri curled up in bed with me, and I saw Jen laying down with her old friend Shane, just about to pass out. Soon after, I put some music on low, continuing to glance up towards her, hoping that she would awaken. A few moments later, she did.

Jen called me up to the bed with her to listen to music. We laid there together in a suspended moment, my head caressed in the crook of her shoulder, while I ran my fingertips across her body, and she played with my hair, kissing my forehead. I leaned up to her shut eyes, looking for permission to kiss her, but I couldn't bring myself to do it, to risk ruining the perfectness of the moment. She asked me to put something on, anything I wanted to listen to. I wasn't sure where to take things. We were both exhausted and on the verge of passing out, and all that I wanted was to put something soothing on that shared my soul so that she could feel what I did. I decided on Liza Minelli's "Gently" album, one which, in a vast library of music, I never really listened to. Because maybe, if I picked a song that couldn't just come on the radio, one that would only be chosen to be played, I could leave the memory in the safety of our secret world rather than in the FM dial of the regular one.

As we lay in bed together, my hand stroking her side, she grabbed a hold of me and nuzzled closer, leaning into my arms. Her fingers rubbed against mine, tangled like that of lovers. As she gripped my hand, my ring dug into the side of my finger, and as she squeezed harder, I kept thinking, "does she know that this hurts, or is she trying to tell me something..." And the music crooned from the small speakers of my laptop:

*"Chances are, 'cause' I wear a silly grin the moment you come into view, chances are you think that I'm in love with you. Just because, my composure sort of slips, the moment that your lips meet mine, chances are you think my heart's your valentine..."* (Liza Minelli and Johnny Matthis "Chances Are").

Scene: *If our love story was ever made into a movie, I could see a record player, with all of its vintage pops and cracks, playing this song, spinning 'round and round in frozen time. And soft light coming through the scene. Blown-out candles, her hand in mine as the room fades to black.*

And on the night went. Moody, heavy, sensual. It was morning, and I was still wrapped in her arms. Shane awoke around six am and stared at me for a moment with confused daggers, seemingly lost on how I ended up laying there with Jen. As she left, half-asleep, I called Jerri to come join us in bed. Now, laying there in the middle of these two beautiful women, I found myself in paradise. Jen awoke gently, but just for a moment, to readjust her body to face me. I placed my hand in hers as she slid our tangled hands underneath herself, against her stomach, and my other hand rested in Jerri's as I softly whispered "I'm in heaven," to which both women smiled with slightly open eyes before falling peacefully back to slumber. We slept the entire day away while Jerri made eggs and bacon in the kitchen, and until Jen's mom came into the room and blatantly stated "I don't think Jerri would be too happy about this." Little did she know...

The day finally had to come to an end. Jen's on-again, off-again ex-girlfriend Chantelle was in the hospital and asked her to bring her some essentials. In addition to this, Jen's mom had felt I had overstayed my welcome, so after receiving a gift of a painting, created by her now world-famous artist-dad, and strangely consisting of two lesbian lovers on a bed (which oddly enough partly resembled myself and his daughter), I hopped into the car, barely hugging Jen goodbye, and Jerri and I headed back to Texas.

And just like that, she was gone; the one thing about this love, it always comes crashing down. So close, and yet so far; so true and yet it's only make-believe. All I know is that this time, there are two contradictory ideologies puzzling around my brain. The first is that drunks and children always tell the truth, the latter is that the drunk persona of an individual does not necessarily reflect the true intentions of said individual. Having said that, I am not quite sure which one is more of a cop-out. The truth of the matter is that isolated events that pivot on a "drunk's truth" can be rationalized as unintended and inebriated spontaneity. Actions that occur repeatedly over the course of years, decades even, cannot be discerned as easily. More so, these impressions are further complicated when you introduce a functioning alcoholic into the mix.

# Chapter 22

# Once Bitten and Twice Shy

## The Cause And The Cure: Clarity

She knows the perfect words to make me fall, again and again. We are like magnets that change poles. Repelling and attracting, in an endless quantum sky. That is the plight of stasis that I hold with Jen. A confusion—a muddle that is both the cause and the cure:

As DJ Zedd puts it:

*"If you pull then I push too deep and I fall right back to you"/*
*"If our love is tragedy, why are you my remedy?"/*
*"If our love's insanity, why are you my clarity?"* (*Clarity* 2012)

---

## To The Woman Who Writes My Body

She consumes me. Not because she means to but because of true love; its passion is fire, and fire consumes. I wake up nights, needing to tell her again: *I write you to dream you.* For her to see me as I am held captive in her heart.

How in every instance of every day I feel her. I see her. I push back these thoughts for only a few hours, if any at all, until they surface again. I want to write her a letter. It would say the following:

*J, I love you. I never stopped loving you. Jen, I am in love with you. I never stopped being in love with you. I have fallen in love with you over and over again throughout a lifetime. I want so desperately to hold you, to kiss you, but I can't because I am only burning embers of frozen time. You bring me butterflies in a text message the same way you have always been able to do in person.*

*You still make my heart race just skirting the edge of what it is that I always want to say. You drive me crazy. You drop me dead. You are the sun, the moon, the stars, the essence of my life and the breath that I breathe. You are the beating of my heart. You are the song running through my mind. You are the wind. You are everything to me. And yet you are not mine. It is at five a.m. that I find myself compelled to say this. And I am saying it as a newly engaged woman.*

*I am, however, not engaged to you*
*And I am in love with her too.*
*What can I do...*

At the conclusion of writing this poem, the phone pings. It's Jen, just saying good morning; her heart is inextricably tied to mine.

# The Mystery of Cell Phones

*There is a strange symbiosis occurring between the ideal of the 'textual' and 'social media-world', and that of the 'real' in the real world. What makes this difficult to navigate is the ability to see language rather than to <u>see</u> it. What I mean is that the text world is interpretive...it lacks connection, emotion, body language, eye contact, and most importantly, an understanding of the depths of sincerity. The Reality: In an instant, one can feel both connected through it, and yet at the same exact moment, detached from it.*

*It, too, is like the wind...*

If I am going to tell the whole story, in the way that my butterfly chrysalis slowly entombed me, I must go back to the words that existed behind the woman. Whether I *wrote her body, or she simply wrote me,* I'll leave that up to you.

The second part of this love affair, the one that changed our once-proclaimed friendship with boundaries into an indefinable lifetime relationship started around 2014. It started with a little flirting and pet names; something just innocent enough to not see the night train coming: After hearing her cry into the phone that to see how she feels about me I would need to watch Orange is the New Black, and after I made the promise to move back to Florida, my phone was ablaze; our relationship, caught in the cyberreality of long-distance romance, was marked with her incessant love bombs and declarations of love:

*"I Heart You. Night babycakes. Happy to hear you are thinking (about moving to) FL again. I got busy here at work. I'll talk to you tonight. Xoxoxoxo"*

On a sober night, just like Lady A (formerly known as Lady Antebellum) asking, *"And I wonder if I ever cross your mind?"* (*Need You Now*), I posed the question to her:

*"You always cross my mind :) even when I'm busy working, sleeping, and living I always think of you."*

And when I ask her about songs—about all the times that she played a song and told me to listen to it, that it was from her to me, that the lyrics were echoing the words of her heart:

Me: *"They're just songs, right?"*

Jen: "Yup... But there's always that *connection* silly."

And on the precipice of declaring our love for one another, while I made the decision of how to tell Jerri, The decision that made me:

Jen: *"I think Jerri is amazing and I would never take you from her. All of us could be a possibility...you're not leaving her. I won't let you."*

And when I asked if she was willing to try—to spend a life with me, to share the rest of her life with me:

Jen: *"Ok, I'm willing dammit. To break everything down and build anew with you."*

And when I ask her about sex, while she is sober again, and I just can't figure out why we have never been there together:

Me: *"How did we never go there...so weird how its so easy to fuck the ones that end up not being right, but it is so hard w the ones who could be...fuck."*

Jen: *"Very deep, but true you know..."*

And even when I asked if she would ever leave me, if I could ever lose her:

Jen: *"I would go to the ends of the earth with you...I'm not going anywhere."*

**And thousands of texts later, she had never taken it back.**

Jen (sober) : *"I love you. And I mean every word I said."*

AND YET...

It was around Fall of this year when I received a text from Jen, which said it all: "I'm sorry honey, I'm not here anymore; that girl is gone." It was on this message that our love receded back into the weeds, as it always does, morphing into the stories of legends, the simultaneous *once-again and never-was* inside her endless hurricane; a force that I could not control but yet it would bend, like so many palm trees, to contradict itself eternally at her will.

But even this wasn't the forever end. We would find ourselves wavering back and forth during the winter months, affectionate over my birthday, when she called me via Skype, and, while I stood there clad in no makeup, my California State University hoodie, and pajama bottoms, and she called me "the most beautiful girl in the world"; and absolutely crushed like dust by April, when she preceded to look me dead in the eyes and scream "Fuck You" a million times over during our Skype session, which broke my heart into a million pieces.

Three words had brought me back to my childhood bliss, two more tore the fabric of my soul and left a broken woman in its place. An eternal paradox.

And even after all this... we still found ourselves texting, on Skype, hanging out and saying everything and nothing at the same time. Jen's inability to communicate her true emotions continued to take its emotional toll on me. Now in the final years of my Masters of Arts Degree, and quickly approaching the conclusion of my work in Secondary Education, I was still navigating the choppy waters of being bonded to a black stallion. Each time that she didn't follow through with our evening plans from long distance, I would burst into tears, partly from not knowing if she was sleeping with anybody else, if she had fallen in love with someone new; part of my pain came from thinking the worst and believing that this was all just shadow games, and part of it remained because I couldn't believe that over twenty years later, this woman could bring me to the precipice of non-stop tears, when the silence became deafening between the days and weeks of our communication and shared time with one another.

AND YET...

Jerri stuck faithfully by my side, nursing the wounds inflicted by my sometimes-sadistic soulmate. And as I spiraled down the abyss of my own ineptitudes and insecurities, I learned a lot about myself over the next year. How far I had come, how much further I needed to go. I recognized every fragment of Jen in myself, in ways that both tortured and terrified me. We knew each other's deepest demons, and yet we were still able to come together and share them all, stars and scars, without judgment. To this day, those confidences will stay part of the sacred space I share with her—a space that I simply could not walk away from—the infinity of unconditional love. But as she slid into the arms of yet another new woman after several years of reaffirming the undying love that we felt for one another, I found myself crumbling again under the weight of her wanton affections. I felt myself slip under the ether over the same negativities that sent me running oh so many years ago. The only difference now was my career as a teacher and my continuing Masters degree, which just piled on top of me, until Jen's simple words became the storm that I couldn't escape from.

But I felt that she tried this time, more than ever before. This time, in giving her credit for not trying to hurt me as bad as she had before, I found my next way out was as simple as hurting myself.

*Get angry. Think mean and horrendous thoughts.* All in an effort to make sure that she didn't cross my mind. Ever. Imagine myself a monster, unworthy of her love, who was only being rejected yet again because I deserved it. *I must have deserved this.* And as I questioned my own sanity, only months after confirming its stability to her, I became lost and despondent in a sea of numbness, watching the anemones swirl inside my head—drowning in thoughts that were not my own. With my anxiety peaking, my OCD pinged, and my world flying out of control, I continued to trek forward in my responsibilities, bearing the cross that I had knowingly placed upon my own shoulders time and time again; one that I had begun to carry so many years before.

And I played the games of my childhood: not speaking, ignoring her, realizing quite quickly that in the few times I had done so that I had pushed the last of her away.

As the silence between us grew further, I found myself fighting the impulse to call and declare my love, like I had always done in the past. Instead, I placed all my pain into the nightmarish thoughts that now reeled in my mind; thoughts of her new lover's intentions, of her own desires, and of the way that I was hopelessly caught in the middle; possibly even a pawn of an evil and otherworldly spiritual game that I knew oh too well.

Fast forward another year or so. Jen and I had only communicated with each other a handful of times that year. I was trying to give her space to let her relationship be her focus. But a year later while Jerri and I were preparing for the happiest day of our lives, Jen's world was crashing down around her. The girlfriend she had gotten with and loved enough to exchange rings had left her on the Fourth of July, taking everything with her from Jen's trailer—including the bed and shower head—just three weeks shy of Jerri and I's wedding day. Jen had moved what little was left out of the trailer that she shared with her now-ex and was living with her mom again. A week later, Jerri and I would be taking our enchanted trip to the beachside oasis that would become the setting for our wedded bliss, and Jen would be spiraling towards her own destruction.

And a week later, as I was pulling up into the parking lot for our hotel, my phone started to go off. It was Jen, begging me to come down to the Wet Spot, our renamed Memory Lane dive bar haunt. I hesitated, having just come in from a twenty-hour drive, until she proceeded to point out that I could "spare an hour for her." So, as soon as we threw our luggage into the room, Jerri and I were off again onto our next three-way adventure.

When we arrived at the bar, Jen was sitting outside with some friends. She got up from her seat, and like a tale out of some romance novel, our eyes locked. I pretended not to notice her, wiping the humidity from my glasses, while she proceeded to look at me in hidden glances. When I came to her, she met me at the table, standing up to embrace me for minutes on end, while everyone around us just sat in a suspended silence. It was only me and her in that moment, and she was holding me so tight, it was as if I had the power to make everything that hurt her go away, if only but for a moment in time. I breathed her in, my face against her neck, her hair, and I was taken aback, far away into a world where it was only us two, until someone snapped me back into my own reality. "Congratulations on the wedding! Jen told us all about it! You and Jerri make a great couple..."

I spent the next hour slamming Jager bombs, while Jen slightly sipped on a beer and washed it down with plenty of water. This was a new M.O. for her, and I kind of liked it. When the bartender shouted last call, I asked if anyone needed anything, and someone in our group randomly called to me to grab a pint. When I asked of what, they responded "Fireball!" Let the good times begin!

One of the perks of being a regular of a bar, and in Jen's case, an ex-bartender, is knowing all the secret spots that the party continues into after the bar closes. As we walked around the building to some benches behind the bar, I knew that this night had something special in store for the three of us—something that I couldn't even imagine. Jerri, Jen, and I drank a lot, then dodged the random people that we were sitting with by going over to Jen's friend Tonya's house, where she proceeded to give Jerri and I a blanket for Jen's cold floor and two small bottles of champagne to celebrate Jerri and I's nuptial day.

Since we planned on staying at Jen's house even before her breakup with her latest girlfriend, we weren't going to let a little thing like a lack of bedding or furniture keep us from having a good time. So to avoid public intoxication charges, Jen decided to take us on a treacherous walk through the pitch-black woods—a hidden path on the shortcut back to her empty home.

Armed only with a cell phone, we battled through the forest, vested with our liquid courage. Forget about bugs, snakes, or any of the multitude of dangers that lurk in a dark forest at four a.m. We walked for what felt like hours, until my foot gave out on a crag-like rock and I came tumbling down like a domino into Jen, whose body broke my fall. As I dusted off my bruised legs and scraped knees, the two loves of my life helped me up, and we made our way over the night train tracks, soon finding ourselves in her backyard.

The evening continued with beers and cheers, reminiscing over music on our phones as we always do. The only problem was that we didn't have any phone chargers in the empty house, so Jen improvised. We sat like hungry children on the front porch steps of her home, yearning for music that would take us back again to our childhood: The Cure's *Disintegration* album, and we sang its lyrics. And this is when I jumped off the metaphorical ledge with an impulsive leap of faith. I looked deep into her eyes and told her "I am going to kiss you now." And this time, it **was** different. I gently cupped my hands around her face, and softly came under and up to her, watching her eyes close, and a soft smile surface on her face. She leaned in. And I kissed her, with a building passion, several times over, until she slipped her tongue in my mouth, this time tender and sweet, mimicking my own kissing style. And I could feel my heartbeat beginning to speed up, as I ran my tongue against hers, kissing her bottom and upper lip; this time not rushing, savoring it. Inhaling her as we pulled our lips apart. And as we opened our eyes together, all I could say was *"Now?"* And she knew exactly what I meant. Jen softly breathed the word '*...don't*' as I sat there, lost in my head at the realness of the moment, and as Jerri came out the screen door, asking if she had interrupted us and if we wanted a minute, the moment passed through us. As it always seems to do. For yet another night of eternity...

Jerri and I ended up back at our hotel around nine a.m., and as I fell asleep in Jerri's arms, I thought about kissing Jen. How this time it was perfect. How I felt the power in that kiss. Each one, for my lifetime, so different. Unique. Memorable. Or how maybe this was a sign that I was making a huge mistake in marrying Jerri. Or maybe, just maybe, that the three of us could actually work. Jerri as my stability, my core. The love I can trust. Strong and giving and so into me sexually that my body rages against her heat at the mere sensation of her touch. And Jen as my endless other, the soulmate I never asked for but bonded with so many decades ago—the woman who forever had my heart. My first true love, and true love's first kiss.

The next few days, Jerri and I slept through the sun and waited for Jen so we could go howl at the moon with her again. And, like clockwork, we found ourselves at Jen's again just a few days later, this time helping her move the remaining possessions that she previously stored at her parent's house back to the same very trailer where she would now return with a roommate and try to live on her own terms. With Jerri's best man Diego in tow, we finished moving the last of the boxes, we cracked open beers, and let the good times roll. I also topped off a bottle of Fireball and waited for the fireworks between Jen and I that I knew were coming.

#The Heart Wants What It Wants

# Chapter 23

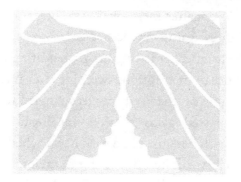

## 'Making Love' Out of Nothing at All...

### Sharing Our Secret World Together

Jen was in a strange state that night, even inviting strangers into her home to cry about her ex with a new ear, and I was getting sick of being ignored by her. When she went into the front room to change the music, I found her laying down by the couch and decided to join her. After whispering in her ear "I don't like that strange lady, please get rid of her" she pulled me in and said "get her out of my house, I don't want her here anymore." We laughed a little as Jen put on DJ Icey's "Escape", one of my favorite technos songs from our raver days. She 'membered'.

I stood up and danced with her for a second, until I felt like sitting, and she gave me a lightshow without glowsticks. I could still feel the sensations of raving in our youth, see the trails of her fingers, and I even 'blew up' a little, just from the thought of her with me in that moment. Chills ran through my body as my eyes rolled to the back of my head. Pure Ecstasy.

We laid back down together against the arm of the couch; Jen put on one of our favorite songs by George Michael's band Wham, "Careless

Whisper"—the same song that played that night in her room, when I came over after Sandy and I had broken up, and she danced with me softly before offering to do anything to make my dreams come true.

Grabbing me at the waist, she pulled me down to the floor with her, grinding her body close against me, violently pulling at my body, squeezing, pushing, leaving bruises against my flesh. I could feel all of her—her hurt, her love, her feelings for me, her letting me go, her bringing me back to her. Everything, like an ocean of emotion, sweeping over me, wave after wave. And we sang, screaming on the floor, her legs tangled with mine; my submissive body tightly pressed against her side, yearning to jump on top of her, play fight, kiss and ravish her; just to be with her. I ached to push her hands behind her head and just take her. But in this moment, her body continued to writhe against me, side to side, as she locked eyes with me and we became lost amid a sexless sexual moment.

I want to capture the truth authentically, which is that we didn't take our physical desires past the point of no return, even though I wanted to— I felt she did too—but we were just lost in our needing and longing for one another; we were right there in the moment, each open for the taking, and breathing heavy on the floor.

The truth about grinding: it is a form of sex, don't let anyone tell you differently. As I lay there with her, feeling her, all of her, the weight against my side, the hands groping, searching my flesh, the kisses and the drunkenness and the friendship and the passing of that line, all I can think in the moment, is that she and I are one. So in this sexless sex, we lie together, sweating in our beer and whiskey blankets, all the while fully clothed and chalked full of awareness at the act we were not performing. Our bodies of light merging, absent of our physical bodies.

Suffering endlessly in this entanglement of our skins, we kissed. Again. And again. But just for a moment, the way we always do. And all while Jerri's best man laid sleeping on the couch, just out of eyeshot from Jen and I writhing against each other, softly moaning and panting on the floor. Our hands intertwined: we held on for dear life, her fingers tracing my veins, her breath hot against my neck. As the song ended, we remembered our main objective: get the strange lady out of the house. So far, Jerri had been able to corner her outside on the patio so she could not come in, but Jen and I knew that we wanted to stay right here, in our moment, so I came up with the idea to play *Last Dance*, by Donna Summers—a song infamously known as a last-call song at bars nationwide. As Donna crooned "Last Dance, last chance, for romance, to-night…" Jen screamed, "*Get out!*"… "for romance, *leave*"… "tonight" … "*go away*." Halfway through the song, Jen crawled on all fours to the wooden floor of the hallway and banging on the ground, bellowed, "*Get out…Get Out!!!*" in a fashion reminiscent of Joan Crawford in "Mommy Dearest."

Finally, a few minutes later, and after the lady left, Jen called Jerri inside. She stood up, sober as a judge, and went back to where we were laying on the floor, intentional and full of fire. And taking me down again with her.

Jerri sat down on the edge of the couch now, leaving the two of us still cuddling together. Jen stretched her legs out against me, as we just drifted into this moment reminiscent of our childhood flirtations, still touching, petting, soft kisses, light embraces. She began stretching her body again, this time proving she was much more flexible than I had remembered; she lay there, putting her foot over her head, limber, agile, making me go crazy. Thoughts racing my mind of what to do with her form. And then I felt her calling to me, saw a light in her eyes as she laid back down and tugged at the waistband of her pajamas, slipping them down ever so slightly, revealing the very edge of herself, her warmth, placing the proverbial ball in my court.

But I could also feel the pain in her eyes. Her breakup with her ex, tearing at her soul. I calmed myself.

*She's drinking. She's hurting. It's not supposed to be like this.* I talked myself out of going too far. I slid over to the left of her, against her right side, as I always do. My need to wait for a sign, for an invite, when in reality, it was right there in front of me.

Then Jen reached out for Jerri's hand, and as I lay there with her, she began running her hands interlacing through Jerri's fingers. I watched them kiss, watched them in their own moment, just taking in the fact that it didn't really bother me. I wanted them to be close. And I wanted to be a part of that moment too. After a few minutes elapsed, I brought my hands into the mix. The three of us held hands, Jen kissing each one, and then placing my hand into Jerri's, entrusting Jerri with something that was precious to her: *Me*. And as we got up to smoke a cigarette after, she grabbed my face between both hands and kissed me again, and I knew something truly sacred, truly special had taken place. In some strange way, Jen had placed her blessing on Jerri and I's union, all the while making love to me, fully clothed, bathed in her glow, and yet far from the physical penetration of the actual act—what separates fantasy from reality. Yet her sex that night penetrated my very soul.

# Chapter 24

# Promises, Promises

### Finding the Words

As the day of our wedding grew closer, Jerri and I were wrapped up in the planning, and Jen had to work most of her nights at the hospital to be able to get the time off for the wedding later that week.

Jerri and I spent the next few days fulfilling the myriad of remaining wedding duties that we couldn't finish in Texas: we tasted gourmet reception appetizers with our friend Chad, did a trial run of my hair with my amazing stylist, and tasted decadent cake samples to decide on the flavors of our wedding cake tiers. In addition, I went clothing shopping for an awesome after-wedding outfit with Jerri's best man and my new friend, Diego, while Jerri worked on setting up outside canopies. Amidst this, we still somehow found time to go and get our flowers and meet with our photographer. Even though everything was going splendidly, at this point, we were exhausted beyond belief, and worn out from all the nights of partying in the exclusive bachelor party that Jen had been throwing for the last few days without us knowing.

As we blew off everyone and cuddled for hours on end, Jerri and I had many conversations—the most notable, a heart-to-heart about the past week with Jen and the future of the indefinable relationship that the three of us had been engaged in for quite a few years now.

This was also the night that Jerri, out of her own love and volition, asked if she could invite Jen to be a part of our marriage union, and if she could seal the deal by designating the three parts of my wedding ring, a three-part piece, as symbolically representing the three of us, with 2 bands around the center, and my diamond, in the middle (because remember, I am the Queen who always sleeps in the middle). I took her in jest, saying "sure, go ahead and do that and see what happens."

Little did I know she would take me seriously... but that comes later.

Meanwhile, the bruises Jen left behind from our tumbling night of passion ringed my body in places I had never known existed. I was sore, hungover—my body broken, my mind racing, and my heart torn. *Four weeks after the wedding, the bruises had only slightly faded, and I was left for a while with a set of markings which reminded me of the love making that both was and never was*—the ring of our triad still weighing heavy on my left hand.

# Chapter 25

# Something Old, Something New

## Making Lifelong Decisions in the Blink of an Eye

How did this all come to be, you might ask? Well, when we initially traveled to Corpus Christi in May to visit Jerri's best man and work on wedding details, we just so happened to go to a shopping outlet, to kill some time and help Diego look for shoes to fulfill his ever-growing foot fetish. It also happened that there was a Kay Jewelers there, so Jerri decided we should go in to look at their wedding band selections. But, when Jerri found out that my engagement ring didn't come with a matching band, she tried endlessly to find a match, until all at once, the right one came to us, and it took my breath away. It wasn't one band after all, but two, that would become soldered to the original ring to give it a glorious symmetry and a one-of-a-kind look.

What I didn't know is what that ring truly meant to Jerri—that in that moment of purchasing that ring, in her heart, she knew that the second band belonged to the second heart that I loved: it belonged to Jen.

This knowledge, however, was unbeknownst to me until a mere 2 days before the wedding. And I wouldn't know how deep this rabbit hole would go until the precious few moments right after the wedding, when Jerri would pull me aside and quickly tell me the story of how I just married her, my wife, and also Jen, my soulmate, in the same wedding vows.

# Love Doesn't Ask Permission

After several failed attempts to have "the talk" Jerri wanted to have with Jen about what had just happened between the three of us, and to tell her what the ring meant, it just didn't seem to be in the cards. Jen was still very heartbroken over her ex, and everytime that we found ourselves alone with her, it was either during some flirtatiously unplanned petting and kissing session, or on the other end of her cold shoulder; we would find ourselves, the three of us, in Jen's bed, together, sleeping; in the morning of her waking, we would find ourselves, again and again, spending endless nights with her, over the few days that we had in town, both before and after Jerri and I shared our nuptial vows.

And then one of the worst possible scenarios happened. The night before the wedding, we both invited Jen over to our Seascape village to join the inner party in celebrating the wedding, and to remind everyone of the now-quickly-approaching timeline of the nine a.m. wedding rehearsal. Jen, after some heavy convincing, finally came over to the Seascape, but not without about seven other strangers in tow. Knowing that this was a private engagement, I could not have been angrier with Jen in all of my life as I was in that moment. Some very unsavory men proceeded to traipse in and out of our open hotel room continuously—a space that we had left open, because, up until that point, we knew and trusted everyone on property as our family and friends.

When we finally kicked her party out, she went home to do things unmentionable and seemingly out of her character—things that I have vowed to keep secret and take to the grave. At first, I thought maybe it was because she was hurting so much about her ex. But there is something to be said of the timing, and the sense that she was hurting about something else... maybe someone else.

Maybe me. And she still didn't know that she was included in everything that was our wedding, right down to the ring on my finger.

She must have felt so alone. Here I was, moving on, living in Texas. And here she was, stuck in Florida in a breakup hell. Or maybe that wasn't really it at all. Maybe, just maybe, all she was worried about was the fact that she was losing me, and our closeness, forever.

So, on the brink of being exiled from the intimacies of our life together, Jen showed up at nine a.m., deep in sunglass shades with both hugs and apologies, and a heartfelt attempt to not ruin one of the most important days of my life. All three of our lives... even if she didn't know it yet.

The next few hours, I was not privy to. So instead of trying to recreate the conversation that changed our lives forever from a second-hand account, I will simply hand the writing reins over for a moment to Jerri, the other half of our third:

*So after the rehearsal wedding, Dolores was going to the hair salon with my sisters Jenna and Becky. Diego had made some plans with Julio, and Chad was a no-show to the rehearsal. I had nothing left that had to be done at that moment, and I had convinced Jen to stay in one of our vacant rooms to rest the night off. I decided to finally have the conversation that had been eating at me for the entirety of the trip. I had tried a few days before, but couldn't muster up the courage to ask her for a moment alone.*

*When I knocked on her door, she was inside with her roommate, whom she promptly sent back to her house to pick up the stuff that she needed to get ready for the wedding. I asked to have a conversation with her alone, and she sat up in the bed and had me sit next to her. I brought the ring box out of my pocket, and told her this:*

*"I wanted to talk to you before the ceremony; I have been wanting to talk to you for a while now. I have known about you for the entirety of our relationship because Dolores has always had a special place in her heart for you. I had two options for this ring: because it does not have a matching wedding band, either get a custom ring made or get two rings to surround the engagement ring. Something told me when I saw the three rings together that it was meant*

*to be that way. Dolores and I have had a few discussions about this, and we wanted to have one of those bands be for you.*

*Also, I have included you as a part of my vows...when you hear me talking about prior relationships that's all you. I am not just marrying Dolores today, I am also marrying the two of you, if you don't mind."*

*At that point Jen gave me a huge smile and a long and heartfelt hug and we proceeded to lay down next to one another and started talking about our future home. And how Chewy our cat and her three dogs would get along, since in the next year we would plan for the three of us to move in together.*

# Our Wedding

Finally, after literal years of preparations, the wedding ceremony was upon us. As I finished up with hair and makeup, Daniel, my man of honor, proceeded to help me into my dress.

One of my absolute favorite moments from the wedding preparation was the act of standing at the mirror, looking at my reflection in the full-length gown, and seeing Daniel behind me, like a doting sister, placing the necklace Jerri had bought to accent the ring, around my neck.

When the wedding was about to begin, Keith, my best friend from California who had flown in to give me away (in place of my deceased father), proceeded to hand me a shot of vodka as a last-minute symbol of the unbroken bonds between us, and the processional began.

Not knowing the earlier intimacies of Jerri's conversation with Jen, I walked down the aisle, slowly, just taking in the moment. While the song I wrote for Jerri played from our P.A. system, the rich tones of her friend Artie's saxophone came crooning through its bridge. Overcome with emotion, Keith walked me to the altar, and that is where I took Jerri's hand. We stood there in the moment, as I looked around me—at all of our friends and family, at the faces of our inner wedding party, and at both of the women whom I loved, and a sense of calm and rightness came over me like a cool breeze. As we stood together with our officiant, I felt every moment resonate in the depths of my heart. And as Jerri and I took each others' hands and said our vows, both written by the other, the same words in each vow echoed the music flowing through our hearts. "I love you theeeesseee much."

## In the Aftermath of Vows

After the ceremony and the photo session, Jerri and I were first approached by Sasha's sister, Shara. She complimented us on the wedding and then directed our attention to the skies. As the three of us looked out onto the ocean horizon, a sign from God had formed in the aftermath of the quick evening shower that had just blown over moments before the wedding—a beautiful rainbow hung from the clouds—and placed a seal of approval on a rare rainbow wedding for two that I never knew until later was really a wedding for three.

Jen left shortly after the photographer shot the wedding party. As we made our rounds, speaking with each of our guests, something felt like it was missing... her.

That was when Jerri pulled me aside and let me know what had transpired there in the moments right before the wedding—the promise that had occurred between the two of them. And as I went through the obligatory cake-cutting and best man speeches, a part of me was already gone, just daydreaming, waiting for the evening to hurry up and come to an end so that Jerri and I could go be with our other wife.

After the impromptu skinny-dip of my new sister Jenna's boyfriend, Jerri and I went out to a bar to celebrate with friends, but we both knew that we wanted to cut the night short and head over to celebrate with Jen. We drank a few shots, danced to a few songs, and then told everyone we were retiring from a long day and late night.

Jerri told me to go up to the door first. As I walked up to Jen's door, I took a good look at myself now, after the wedding, dressed down in a beautiful white silk blouse, comfortable black pants, and a matching black hat and tie. Having changed from my feminine wedding dress, I now felt the aspects of my androgyny return to me, subtle in their feminine form, and yet asserting a masculinity which felt familiar: I wanted to take charge, desiring to be the one who finally made the full move towards Jen that would set the three of our orbiting planets in motion.

Jen was already sitting cross-legged in her pajamas on the patio, balancing on a chair, as Jerri and I walked through the door and the three of us deeply embraced.

We sat down together and poured a glass of cheap champagne from yet another small bottle which had been given to us the night before, and we toasted the moment between the three of us, along with Jen's old flame Chantelle. As we sipped our celebration from the same single ceremonious wine glass, it was a powerful moment of womanhood: bonding, embracing, even vulnerably breaking down under the now-released pressure of too many stressors for the last few weeks—work, school, wedding planning, Jen's unspoken spoken, and the bustle of everyday life. But Jen was not the receptive lover that I had embraced just a few days ago: replaced in her now was a more prominent ache for her ex to return, a desire that I had only subdued for a short while in our last week's reunion. I felt myself spiraling downward into this loss, confusing, confessing, crashing into all of my insecurities, overthinking and unable to control the sense of panic and impending doom that had now replaced my happiness. I needed to talk to Jen, but I didn't know how to begin; how to place what happened just a few hours ago into the conversation, while she sat and spoke to me of wanting desperately to get back with her ex, whom she was still in love with.

Instead of talking to her, I found myself sitting with the long ashes at the tip of my cigarette, trying to reconcile her coldness, and, mentally worn out, I avoided the conversation altogether; instead, I was in the other room, shading an adult coloring book, avoiding Jen while getting my tarot read by Chantelle, all the while holding back the emergent need to wrap Jen in my arms, to hold her tight, and to seal our new wedding pact with the softness of a marital kiss, and the possible consummation of our vows.

But she was not having it. I could read her signals and see that she did not want this. I felt trapped inside my own mind now, my own emotions and mental stability pivoting on that of my soulmate's. I had been at the top of the mountain to know what Jerri had confided in her that evening, and what she had confessed in return. But like the ocean tides, with the highs, comes the lows.

As I sat outside, smoking endless cigarettes, Jen retired to the bedroom. Moments later, I looked over to Chantelle and told her, boldly, "Jen asked me to come over and spend the night with her." Chantelle looked me dead in the eyes, and with the tender release of an ex lover, she said "Then what are you still doing here? Go to her."

And that is precisely what I did. But laying in Jen's bed that evening felt almost obligatory. I was nervous and frustrated and wanted to just say everything, but the words wouldn't come out. I reached my arm out to hold her hand, Jerri to the left and Jen to the right, and she pulled away, ripping my heart once again from inside my chest. I got up for a moment to freshen up, and from the room next door, I could hear Jerri saying to her, point blank: "if you wanna keep Dolores from freaking out about this, you have to reciprocate." When I returned, I made sure not to get too close, relinquishing myself to the middle of the bed, until, surprisingly, she took my hand under the pillow, and intertwined it with hers.

And then again, just as quick as it was starting, it ended. We left Florida the next day, having barely given each other a hug—the pull away maneuver that we both knew all too well, where we would act like it didn't hurt, it wasn't a big deal, we were just friends who would have to wait to see each other again for a while. No biggie.

And life went on again, not speaking but a few words to each other, texts that were rushed, attempts to video chat that failed. Jen spent her time trying to keep herself together, and I spent my time hurting over how yet again we were falling apart. Until the next time that I would find myself in her world.

#TheHeartWantsWhatItWants

# Chapter 26

## New Years is for Lovers

### Retying the Not

I spent the last six months delving into my job, trying to get situated in my thesis work for my Masters, and devoting every spare minute that I had to keeping the quasi-matrimonial bond as tight as I could between Jen, Jerri, and myself. And as soon as I could blink, there was a new woman in Jen's arms—Vanessa.

At first, I thought this could be a good thing. Jen introduced me to Vanessa one night over Skype and we seemed to hit it off. But when, after nights of binge drinking and the added confusion of Jen's new attempt at a relationship, I found myself worried not only for her heart but for her health, Jerri and I made a last-minute decision to visit her on New Years. Not sure what to make of the trip, I kept my heart reserved, reminding myself that I was more concerned about Jen being okay than for me. I even fought against the timing: after all, the last thing I wanted to do over my short break from work was to end up at a New Year's party or bar hopping for the duration of my short three-day stent, when all I wanted was to see how Jen was, how she was living, and where our place was in her life now.

So, when after being in town for only a few hours, the invitation to go to the bar fell into our laps, Jerri and I recoiled into Jen's room, minus Jen, to attempt to get some rest after our tiring plane ride. We did agree, however, to join Jen and the possible amassing of party goers at the bar after taking a short nap.

## Breaking Up and Making Up Through Confusion and Miscommunication

Jen called about an hour later, to let us know that she was coming home. The reason? A woman at the bar was maddogging her, following her into the bathroom and becoming increasingly violent because she swore they had shared something together in a drunken night at the bar. Jen, on the other hand, didn't even remember her name. The old Jen would have gone off and broken the bar, and her nose, but the new Jen chose to leave, and this was a great first step. So, only returning with one of her close male friends, she proceeded to make the night about what it should be—celebrating the return of her wives to take care of her and celebrate our love together.

Or so I thought.

A few hours later, the world was colored in a glow of near-full moonlight and Jen and I sat next to the fire, talking like old friends who hadn't missed a beat and drinking while reminiscing and watching the chaos of her life unfold. After we had a long talk about the way that she likes to be controlled in bed about a week ago; the way that she was shy and needed someone to make the first move, I chose to finally be brazen enough to make it. To control her. And as Joan Jett played over the speakers, I grabbed her and pulled her in and went for the kiss.

And that's when she pushed my face away.

Broken-hearted, pissed off, I resolved to not cry in front of her. Instead, I walked to the liquor store down the street, buying the biggest bottle of Fireball that they had and getting ready to make things real interesting when I returned.

I loved her. I wasn't going to go out and do something else, but I just couldn't be in that house anymore without my liquid courage. About a half hour later, as I re-entered the home, she acted as if nothing happened, and I walked over to Jen's chain link fence, grabbing ahold of it, looking at the sky, and feeling the weight in my body become too much to bear as I pulled at the taut metal, diamond-shaped bars, pressing them between my hands.

I decided to sit down on the grass, away from the party, away from Jerri and Jen, and just stare into the sky. The moon was cresting over clouds, and my life felt utterly hopeless. Here I am, finally attempting to be the one who makes that move, and she rejects me. Like the millions of times before. And, having lost the will to even move my body, I fell down onto the ground and raised my hands, my fingers locked in a diamond shape, placing them in front of my face, to view through them the circle of the moon. And as I looked at the set of three stars to the direct right of it, Jen came to me and asked if she could join me.

I thought "Here we go. Some excuse. Some explanation. Something that would change the course of our relationship forever. But what could she say? The wife who wouldn't kiss me? And then Jerri came to lay down to my right. As we laid there looking at the sky together, I can't remember what we said. All I know is that both of them kept looking at their watches. And when the clock struck 12:00, I found myself engaged in a passionate three-way kiss-turned-makeout session with Jen and Jerri both—one that Jen herself initiated—grabbing hold of each other and kissing like love drunk fools.

This was the world as it unfolded in 2018. Our promise, our vows, seemed to be coming into fruition. Everything that I had felt up until that moment was encapsulated in that kiss. All the pain, the rejection, the hurt from deep inside me, all came welling out in the deepness of those kisses. And Jerri looked at me and smiled—whispering in my ear: "See, I told you. She loves us. Very much. She just wanted to start the New Year off with her wives, and she was waiting until midnight for that kiss."

And so the night truly began. Jen's friend went and passed out on the couch, and I proceeded to grab a beer instead of my Romeo and Juliet-esque bottle of Fireball 'hemlock.' As I went to take my first swig, Jen slammed her beer on top of mine, the way we did when we were just kids, trying to get me to take it all down. However, in the heat of the moment, with the passion that still burned between us, she ended up breaking the bottle top I was to drink from. If only I had known it before I took that first chug...

As my lips were pierced by the bottle, she quickly knocked it out of my hand, spraying beer everywhere, and I went into semi-shock. The next thing I remember was Jen holding a pack of ice in a paper towel up to my lip, moving it ever so slightly to check the bleeding. Luckily, I had not swallowed any glass, but I was still bleeding profusely. The alcohol consumption had thinned out my blood. Jen was blotting my lip for many minutes, and then she kissed my bleeding lip; the last thing I remember saying then was 'I think I lost a liter of blood' before they both laughed at me, told me it wasn't that big of a deal, and showed me the bloody rag that only had a few splotches. The bleeding had finally stopped.

Now that we had finally taken care of the emergency, Jerri entrusted me to Jen as she too went to bed. And this is when things got real.

## Drunken Confessions and Caught Up Riding Fine Lines

Over the night, we talked about our vows. We discussed whether they were real, why she said them. And she told me how much she loves me, how she loves Jerri, how this could work, and how happy she was that I came out to see her. And then she told me she was dying.

She has said it a few times over the last few months. A few years ago, I even asked her if she was sick. I knew something was wrong but I didn't think she was dying. She can't. I love her too much. She says her blood work was off when she went for a check-up and that there is a mass in her back that won't go away and hurts every day. And as I ran my finger over it, I came up with a thousand things it could be, anything but what she thinks it might be—the Big C.

And when she came up to me, wanting to kiss me again that night, I now cowered, because I could remember this having happened before, having been this close to her, and having her reject me; as a child, saying she wasn't attracted to me physically. As an adult, saying she didn't feel the same way. And I was hurting because she said she was dying. She went to get a drink and clean up. As I sat down on the stoop of her back porch, she finished up in the kitchen, and wiped her wet hands against my lips, kissing them yet again.

And then, she came outside in her leather jacket and got down on the ground, perched in a position that practically brought her to one knee and asked me to look at her. At first, I couldn't. Even though, over the last few months, I had told her she wouldn't make sustained eye contact with me, now it was my turn to have trouble looking at her. I couldn't bring myself to follow her eyes because they were hypnotizing. Enchanting. And I didn't know whether to believe her or not.

"Now who won't look at who? You won't look at me..." she said, as she gently cupped my face in her hands and my eyes leaned up slowly to meet hers.

"I'm a dick. I always have been. But I will never hurt you again. I promise." And with that, she kissed me again, this time, pulling me seriously tight, her kisses like wine against my lips. No tongue this time, only a deep passionate kissing that breathed her into me. Longer, still longer, then any of our kisses before, she ended her passion by sucking on my bottom lip the same way I had hers so many years ago; I felt like a wife whose husband cheated on them over and over again, but deep inside, still had the most deep and ultimate love for her. Even if, like the Sublime song goes, *"He spreads his lovin' all over and when he gets home there's none left for me"* (Sublime, *Doin' Time*). And I'm reminded of the words she used everytime in the past... to let me down gently or to tell me the truth. Maybe to love me so much that she would spare my heart by being the very one to break it:

- From the first time, in my youth:

*"I did what I did to protect you because I love you... no one can ever break your heart this much ever again"*

187

- To the night when she kissed my tears away, after my breakup with Sandy in my early twenties:

*"I let you go because you deserve better than me... You deserve to be happy...."*

- From my early thirties, when, after coming back together again, I would question how she could love me so deeply and still let me go:

*"..."*

- And even in my now 40s, when she tells me:

*"I will love you forever; You belong to me,"* echoing the same sentiments on the very same night when the three of us sealed our mutual fates in each other:

*See the pyramids along the Nile*
*Watch the sun rise on a tropic isle*
*Just remember, darling, all the while*
*You belong to me*

*See the marketplace in old Algiers*
*Send me photographs and souvenirs*
*Just remember when a dream appears*
*You belong to me*

*I'll be so alone without you*
*Maybe you'll be lonesome too, and blue*

*Fly the ocean in a silver plane*
*See the jungle when it's wet with rain*
*Just remember till you're home again*
*You belong to me*

(Jo Stafford, "You Belong to Me" 1952).

So, we were back to where it always began. Where we always began. The two of us, kissing, only once a night. Until it was two times. Until it was three...or five...or ten. Until all I could remember of this night or that was us kissing, over and over again, until my lips were raw, and I finally realized that we were inches away from finally taking our love to the next level.

And that's when she woke up her friend to come and help her build a fire. And as I waited for her to completely tear apart a chair that she had already started to burn in the fire a few nights ago, listening to George Strait's "The Chair" before we arrived, I told her I was going to finally lay down with Jerri and that she should come to bed too. At first, she said she wanted to join us. And we smoked a cigarette and she cracked a beer, and within a few minutes she had completely changed her mind. She was going to stay up. I simply couldn't. Her and her friend worked on getting a new fire going without firewood or flame. She even went so far as to make a makeshift crack lighter so that she could get a flame high enough that would catch off of a spare piece of cardboard from the first empty case of beer that we tossed in the pit. And as much as I wanted to stay up, as much as I wanted to continue what we were doing, I just couldn't hang without some sleep. When I went in to tell Jerri everything that was happening, I heard her snoring, and simply kept the night to myself, curling up in her arms and attempting to get some shut eye.

But who can sleep when the love of their life is sitting outside, still wide awake and heavy with mood? She had taken a walk down to her parents to get gasoline for the fire, and that was just too much for me. When I saw that she was going to burn that chair come hell or high water, I had retreated to bed. But when she returned, with the music blaring and the fire roaring, I simply couldn't miss a moment. I brought myself back outside and watched her continue to drink, and I attempted to do the same, as the half bottles I was actually drinking began to mount up.

And then we both finally rested. We laid down on the couch, but in separate areas, blankets creating oceans between each other. We sat up, not able to sleep, laughing like hyenas. Feeling our friendship returning to where it began as we talked all morning, the one thing that we kept disappearing into the shadows of our almost lovemaking, our friendship. And as we cycled through endless songs on the radio, love songs that brought us both to our knees, and spiritual songs which activated the soulmate bond in both of us, we sang and loved and remembered the other side to all of this.

Her landlord showed up unexpectedly to do some housework, even on New Year's Day. As we were in the process of screaming at the top of our lungs for her Alexa speaker to stop playing a song we had grown tired of, he walked through the door and saw our hung over and mangled asses laughing like misfits on the couch. And we couldn't stop laughing for thirty minutes, even after he left.

As the night finally came down to a close, Jen decided to send her ex a thank you text for every time that someone had died or something bad had happened in life. And then after a few moments, the texts got even more random:

"*Thank you, ex. I'm drunk. Thank you, ex, my girlfriend isn't here because of you. Thank you, ex. Cigarettes cause cancer...*" and so on, over and over, for hours on end.

Playing her games, I told her she should text her from work the next time and tell her that there was a horrible accident at the hospital with mass casualties. And then she should text her every few minutes "...thank you ex...thank you ex...thank you thank you thank you (when the hypothetical family of three passed all together at once), and so on. We were definitely up to no good. And this is when we began to get weak and beyond sick, and the world turned into our own personal hell.

Alcohol poisoning consumed us. I began to get so sick, my head pounding, my back and foot hurting, that I started to hallucinate. Laying on the couch, I remember the body sensation of tripping on LSD right before seeing a vividly colored city with clouds rolling over it, tearing apart like a burn in a movie reel at an old-fashioned theatre. And as I went to ask Jen, my personal nurse for the night, how that was possible, why that was happening, she began to fall into a semi-peaceful slumber. I let it be.

## Making a House a Home: Good Food, Great Conversation, and Loads of Laughter

As we both came back to reality, Jerri having come out to hold me on the couch, me watching a binge of "Shameless" on Netflix, the world seemed right again. Here I was with this woman I was desperately in love with and having gone as far into this relationship as we ever had really gone before. I just took in the moment.

Jerri woke up a few hours later and began frantically cooking for Jen. She brought out a single plate with two forks and what amounted to a seven-course dinner, to show Jen all the yummy food she had made for her to make sure she was eating. We realized that the reason she was not eating very well was because she was not a very good cook, and even though she had massive amounts of food in her fridge, it sat there untouched because she was too drunk most nights to separate, de-thaw, and cook it. Jerri made her enough food for a month, and after cooking for almost eleven hours, we felt as if this whole wives' thing living together could work.

We spent most of the next day recovering, and the final day doing the same. I woke up in the morning on the last day, terrified that I only had a few hours left with my love, and I curled up on top of the blanket Jen was wrapped in, laying on her lap and rubbing her leg. I began to play songs for her that I knew would say the things I wasn't saying last night, because then all I was doing was feeling whatever it was that was coming from her, whatever it was that she wanted me to feel from her and for her. I started with an acoustic cover of Bob Dylan's "To Make You Feel My Love" and moved into Ed Sheeran's "Thinking Out Loud", and then Adele's "A Million Years Ago." Those were the main songs flowing through my heart, and their words, their lyrics, so true of the way I felt with her: Dylan spoke of her having not fully *made her mind up yet* (Bob Dylan, *Make You Feel My Love)*, Ed Sheeran, saying *"baby my heart could still fall as hard at 23... honey now, take me into your loving arms/kiss me under the light of a thousand stars/ place your head on my beating heart"* (*Thinking Out Loud*), and even Adele crooning that *"Life was a party to be thrown, but that was a million years ago"* (Adele, *Million Years Ago*).

And when she stirred from her slumber, I asked her if I woke her up, and she softly said "No. I was actually listening to what you were playing". Because that is what we do. We talk in music and in riddles and we steal midnight kisses and dance in the stars. And when she drove us to the airport, leaving a little bit early so that she would not be stuck driving home all alone in the dark, I continued to think 'what if this is the last time that I see her? What if she regrets that drunken night? Why did I have to fall asleep...'

We hadn't touched since that night, and two days later, her distance from me sober made me question her attraction drunk. But, as we pulled up to the airport, I cooly said to her "do you want to get out or just give us hugs from here?" she replied, "no, I'm getting out to give you each a kiss and a hug." And as she kissed and hugged both of us goodbye, she left me with the hope of a New Year, continuing this journey with the two women I love.

So much so that when I walked into the airport, I was not crying about leaving again, but heady and walking on cloud nine simply because I knew in six months, I might finally be with her for good. And even standing there with a busted lip, at this point, I knew she would never hurt me again. Ever.

Until she broke my heart again for what might be the very last time. In an impromptu conversation before she went to work the very next day, Jerri texted her that I called her name out in my dreams. What she didn't tell her is that I made it all of a two-hour plane ride and twenty minutes away from home, until the feelings of love and lust for her and Jerri were mingling in my head again—so much so, that I had Jerri help undo my belt while she was driving us home. I proceeded to unzip my jeans, frantically panting in a slumped position with one hand draped around the headrest and the other taking care of built up sexual tensions that had been torturing me for three whole days....

# Chapter 27

# Recovering the Black Box

**B**ut I digress. Instead, I will finish, simply by quoting Joseph Campbell in the rendering of my own soul: *"All the gods. All the heavens, all the hells, are within you"* (Campbell *The Power of Myth*).

After telling Jen that I fought back several impulses that next day to grab her in my arms, or the many times I followed her eyes and then cowered as she attempted to walk up to me, wanting to pull her down on the couch, she completely changed tune:

*"D, I've told you that I do not see you in a sexual way. When I get drunk, I do things that I would never do sober."*

And on and on ad nauseum for several hours she would text me about how she doesn't look at me that way, doesn't find me attractive, just acts that way when she's drunk, (blah blah blah)".

And my final checkmate to those words cut so deep, even to this day, that they make me run towards a bottle, make me think about cutting my veins with a knife or the shards of broken glass—the fragments of my broken heart shattering. I think of bleeding out in a bathtub, flaying my skin, my blood, my bone bare in the scars of our love:

"If you know that you fuck around with me drunk and don't wanna be with me sober, then why am **I** the one that you always want to start off drinking with and end the night with? Why am **I** the one who you choose to do this with, time and time again, when you know how I feel about you, and I thought I knew how you felt about me? Why am **I the one that you said you remembered saying you were always in love with** the night that you got too drunk, but you've never taken it back? **And why am I the one that you accepted wedding vows from?**"

## And This is the End (?)

But I wear this ring. I wear it on my finger as a constant reminder of that promise that I was not privy to and yet was a direct part of. And just when I think it's great, she runs to another lover. And just when I think it's over, she finds her way back to me. And this seesaw of a relationship, one that sits in the gray area of blurred borders and crossed boundaries, becomes more real every time that I step inside and then outside of myself. It is both magnified and muted in the depths of her eyes. And we find ourselves talking about dreams, about building a life together, the three of us.

Her heart, beating next to mine, is the only one in the universe which sings my love language, as we suspend time in kissing and song lyrics, in memories and in words, and I am forever taken.

I sit here even now, insecure, wondering how and *if* I will fuck this up, if there is anything left to give—if there is anything left in the wreckage. But when I am with her, it all makes sense again. I love her and Jerri both. And I will have to navigate these uncharted waters of polyamory, for to not try would be to regret my life forever, and what I have always prophesied that it would be—me and her till the end; ride or die. The only difference now is that I brought along an amazing life partner for the ride.

I must go now, as I plan my sojourn back to the woman whom I belong to, who can make my days dark as night and my nights bright as day. To the woman who holds the keys to my heart and decides with perfect indecision, whether to use them like a lover or a jail warden. And as I close this chapter,

I want to share a new tradition that started the night I typed this page. Every time we text, I make sure to say I love you, goodnight, and sweet dreams. A few days ago, Jen decided to use a euphemism she heard from a friend: "*Nite Nite Termite,*" and I immediately thought the worst... until I realized that it was just an endearing way to say goodnight to a loved one you cherish—a phrase used by mothers as they tuck their children into bed. And I worked very hard to find the response to reciprocate this affectionately woven tapestry of words. My choice? "*Good night, love bite.*" Once bitten and twice shy.

*And I want to hold her close; I wanna rip her clothes off.*
*I want to sink my teeth into her flesh and hold on for dear life.*
*I want to be able to feel her, to feel me again.*

# Discography

**Singles:**

2 Live Crew. "Me So Horny." *We Want Some Pussy*. Pac Jam Publishing, 1988.

2 Live Crew. "Pop that Coochie." *Sports Weekend: As Nasty As They Wanna Be, Pt. 2*
Luke Records, 1991.

Adele. "Million Years Ago." *25*. XL, 2015.

Aldean, Jason. "Do You Wish it Was Me." *Relentless*. Broken Bow Records, 2007.

Alice Deejay. "Better Off Alone." *Who Needs Guitars Anyway?* Violent Records, 1999.

Beach Boys. "Surfer Girl." *Surfer Girl*. Capitol Records, 1963.

Belle, Regina and Bryson, Peabo, lyricist. "A Whole New World." *Aladdin*, music by Alan
Menken and Tim Rice. Disney, 1992.

Boyz II Men. "On Bended Knee." *II*. Motown, 1994.

Boyz II Men. "Silent Night." *Christmas Interpretations*. Motown, 1993.

Chicago. "Will You Still Love Me?" *Chicago 18*. Warner Bros. Records, 1986.

Clarkson, Kelly. "Darkside." *Stronger*. RCA/19 Recordings, 2011.

Cole, Nat King. "Unforgettable." *Unforgettable*. Capitol Records, 1954.

Currington, Brady. "Must Be Doing Something Right." *Doin' Something Right*. Mercury
Nashville, 2005.

The Doors. "Stoned Immaculate." *An American Prayer*. Elektra Records, 1978.

DJ Icey. "Beachball." original by Nalin and Kane. Superfly Records, 1999.

DJ Icey. "Escape." *Essential Mix*. original by Kay Cee. London-Sire Records, 2000.

DJ X. "Use Your Luv (R-Fresh and Infiniti Remix)." 12" inch vinyl.
Fresh Productions, 2001.

Etheridge, Melissa. "Come to My Window." *Yes I Am*. Island Records, 1993.

Garbage. "Stroke of Luck." *Garbage*. Almo Sounds, 1995.

Gravediggaz. "Unexplained/Twelve Jewels." *The Pick, The Sickle, and the Shovel*.
12" inch vinyl, white label. Gee Street, 1997.

Hall and Oates. "Sara Smile." *Daryl Hall and John Oates*. RCA Victor, 1975.

Hole. "Miss World." *Live Through This*. Tim/Kerr Records, 1993.

Jackson, Janet. "That's the Way Love Goes." *Janet*. Virgin Records, 1993.

Jars of Clay. "Sinking." *Jars of Clay*. Essential Records, 1995.

Jeremih. "Birthday Sex." Jeremih. Def Jam Recordings, 2009.

Journey. "Separate Ways (Worlds Apart)." *Frontiers.* Columbia, 1983.

Lady A. "Need You Now." *Need You Now.* Capitol Records Nashville, 2010.

Led Zeppelin . "Stairway to Heaven." *Led Zeppelin IV.* Atlantic Records, 1971.

Lords of Acid. "Voodoo-U." *Voodoo-U.* Metropolis Records, 1994.

McLean, Don. "American Pie." *American Pie.* United Artist Records, 1971.

Meyers, Jonathan Rhys, lyricist. "Moondance." *August Rush,* music by Van Morrison.
     Sony Music, 2007.

Mountain. "Mississippi Queen." *Climbing!* Windfall Records, 1970.

Ortopilot. "Make You Feel My Love." original by Bob Dylan. *YouTube,* 2011, https://
     www.youtube.com/watch?v=sv2tHHAdfbQ

Richard Humpty Vission. "Last Night a DJ Saved My Life." original. by Unknown DJS.
     *Shut the Fuck Up and Dance.* Tommy Boy Silver Label, 2000.

Rogers, Kenny. "Lady." *Kenny Rogers Greatest Hits.* composed by Lionel Richie. Liberty,
     1980.

Sheeran, Ed. "Thinking Out Loud" *x.* Asylum/Atlantic, 2014.

Spears, Brittany. "Toxic" *In The Zone.* Jive Records, 2004.

Stafford, Jo. "You Belong to Me." 10" inch, 78 RPM Single. Columbia Records, 1952.

Strait, George. "The Chair." *Something Special.* MCA, 1985.

Sublime. "Doin Time." *Sublime.* MCA, 1996.

Summers, Donna. "Last Dance." *Thank God It's Friday.* Casablanca , 1978.

TLC. "Kick Your Game." *CrazySexyCool.* LaFace/Arista, 1995.

The Verve. "Bittersweet Symphony." *Urban Hymns.* Hut Recordings, 1998.

Wham (by George Michael). "Careless Whisper." *Make It Big.* Epic Records, 1984.

Willie Mix and Darrell Nutt. "Without You." *Dave London: Orlando Breakz Vol. 3.*
     Phattraxx Records, 2001.

Zedd. "Clarity." *Clarity.* Interscope Records, 2012.


**Albums:**

The Cure. *Disintegration.* Elektra Records, 1989.

Minelli, Liza. *Gently.* Angel Records, 1996.

Pink Floyd. *The Wall.* Harvest/Columbia Records, 1979.

West, Rick. *Flavored Beats 4.* Painted Puppy Productions, 1999.

**Additional Attribution Credits:** https://www.photoshopsupply.com/circle-font /
pg#81

# About The Author

Dolores Batten, a Professor/English Lecturer, currently serves as the Senior Essay Editor for Plath Profiles academic journal. With a M.A. in Literature and Language from St. Mary's University in San Antonio, TX, and currently pursuing a PhD at the University of Central Florida in the Texts and Technology program, Dolores's passion for writing has earned her recognition in numerous academic publications and conferences.

This captivating narrative non-fiction work is the result of years of dedicated experience. It chronicles the journey of a young lesbian across the highs and lows of navigating the world as an emerging member of the LGBT community in the United States during the less accepting 1990s. The story is a heartfelt autobiography that delves into the depths of personal growth and relationships. It provokes important considerations and discussions on religion, philosophy, social culture, and the psychoanalytical perspective, all from the unique position of her own personal account. As both an academic and a writer, Batten has skillfully intertwined critical analysis and personal recollections in an ethnography of the first 40 years of her life. This novel offers a universal glimpse into the human condition, exploring emotions that resonate within both the homosexual community and the wider social world.

Printed in the USA
CPSIA information can be obtained
at www.ICGtesting.com
JSHW011112130624
64637JS00013B/98

9 781949 105520